Microsoft®
Publisher® 2000
At a
Glance

KT-476-715

Microsoft Press

Microsoft Publisher 2000 At a Glance

PUBLISHED by **Microsoft Press**
A Division of Microsoft Corporation
One Microsoft Way
Redmond, Washington 98052-6399

Library of Congress Cataloging-in-Publication Data
Microsoft Publisher 2000 At a Glance. Perspection, Inc.
     p.   cm.
   Includes index.
   ISBN 1-57231-950-X
    1. Microsoft Publisher (Computer file)   2. Computer graphics.   I. Perspection, Inc.
  T385.M52225   1999
  006.6'869—dc21
                                         98-48186
                                           CIP

Printed and bound in the United States of America.

1 2 3 4 5 6 7 8 9   WCWC   4 3 2 1 0 9

Distributed in Canada by ITP Nelson, a division of Thomson Canada limited.

A CIP catalog record for this book is available from the British Library.

Microsoft Press books are available through booksellers and distributors worldwide. For further information about international editions, contact your local Microsoft Corporation office. Or contact Microsoft Press International directly at fax (425) 936-7329. Visit our Web site at mspress.microsoft.com.

For Perspection, Inc.
Writers: Elizabeth Reding; Robin Romer; Marie Swanson
Managing Editor: Steven M. Johnson
Series Editor: Jane E. Pedicini
Production Editor: David W. Beskeen
Developmental Editor: Lisa Ruffolo
Technical Editors: Tracy Teyler; Gary Bellig

For Microsoft Press
Acquisitions Editors: Susanne Forderer
Project Editor: Jenny Moss Benson;
                  Kristen Weatherby

Contents

Start Publisher.
See page 6

Get Help with the
Office Assistant.
See page 20

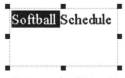

Enter and edit text.
See page 29

Create bulleted lists.
See page 54

One way to achieve a formal and creative look in a publication is to use a dropped capital letter at the start of a paragraph.

Create a dropped
capital letter.
See page 60

Insert pages.
See page 68

Create a table of contents.
See page 83

Crop an image.
See page 89

Choose a color scheme.
See page 106

Crreate WordArt.
See page 120

"How do I create a new table?"

See page 139

Create a publication quickly.
See page 156

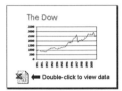

Use smart objects.
See page 168

The Dow

Double-click to view data

Embed an object.
See page 182

"How can I modify a form control?"

See page 202

Create a merged label.
See page 226

"How can I print color separations?"

See page 237

Acknowledgments

The task of creating any book requires the talents of many hardworking people pulling together to meet almost impossible demands. For their effort and commitment, we'd like to thank the outstanding team responsible for making this book possible: the writers, Elizabeth Reding, Robin Romer, and Marie Swanson; the developmental editor, Lisa Ruffolo of The Software Resource; the technical editors and production team, Gary Bellig and Tracy Teyler; and the indexer, Michael Brackney.

At Microsoft Press, we'd like to thank Susanne Forderer for the opportunity to undertake this project, and Jenny Benson and Kristen Weatherby for project editing and overall help when needed most.

Perspection

Perspection

Perspection, Inc., is a software training company committed to providing information to help people communicate, make decisions, and solve problems. Perspection writes and produces software training books, and develops interactive multimedia applications for Windows-based and Macintosh personal computers.

Microsoft Publisher 2000 At a Glance incorporates Perspection's training expertise to ensure that you'll receive the maximum return on your time. With this straight-forward, easy-to-read reference tool, you'll get the information you need when you need it. You'll focus on the skills that increase productivity while working at your own pace and convenience.

We invite you to visit the Perspection World Wide Web site. You can visit us at:

http://www.perspection.com

You'll find descriptions of all of our books, additional content for our books, information about Perspection, and much more.

About This Book

Microsoft *Publisher 2000 At a Glance* is for anyone who wants to get the most from their software with the least amount of time and effort. We think you'll find this book to be a straightforward, easy-to-read, and easy-to-use reference tool. With the premise that your computer should work for you, not you for it, this book's purpose is to help you get your work done quickly and efficiently so that you take advantage of Microsoft Publisher 2000 while using your computer and its software to the max.

No Computerese!

Let's face it—when there's a task you don't know how to do but you need to get it done in a hurry, or when you're stuck in the middle of a task and can't figure out what to do next, there's nothing more frustrating than having to read page after page of technical background material. You want the information you need—nothing more, nothing less—and you want it now! And the information should be easy to find and understand.

That's what this book is all about. It's written in plain English—no technical jargon and no computerese. There's no single task in the book that takes more than two pages. Just look up the task in the index or the table of contents, turn to the page, and there it is. Each task introduction gives you information that is essential to performing the task, suggesting situations in which you can use the task, or providing examples of the benefit you gain from completing the procedure. The task itself is laid out step by step and accompanied by a graphic that adds visual clarity. Just read the introduction, follow the steps, look at the illustrations, and get your work done with a minimum of hassle.

You may want to turn to another task if the one you're working on has a "See Also" in the left column. Because there's a lot of overlap among tasks, we didn't want to keep repeating ourselves; you might find more elementary or more advanced tasks laid out on the pages referenced. We wanted to bring you through the tasks in such a way that they would make sense to you. We've also added some useful tips here and there and offered a "Try This" once in a while to give you a context in which to use the task. But, by and large, we've tried to remain true to the heart and soul of the book, which is that information you need should be available to you *at a glance*.

What's New

If you're looking for what's new in Publisher 2000, just look for our new icon: **New**2000. We've inserted it throughout this book. You will find the new icon in the table of contents so you can quickly and easily identify new or improved features in Publisher. You will also find the new icon on the first page of each section. There it will serve as a handy reminder of the latest improvements in Publisher as you move from one task to another.

Useful Tasks...

Whether you use Publisher for work, play, or some of each, we've tried to pack this book with procedures for everything we could think of that you might want to do, from the simplest tasks to some of the more esoteric ones.

...And the Easiest Way to Do Them

Another thing we've tried to do in *Microsoft Publisher 2000 At a Glance* is to find and document the easiest way to accomplish a task. Publisher often provides many ways to accomplish a single result, which can be daunting or delightful, depending on the way you like to work. If you tend to stick with one favorite and familiar approach, we think the methods described in this book are the way to go. If you prefer to try out alternative techniques, go ahead! The intuitiveness of Publisher invites exploration, and you're likely to discover ways of doing things that you think are easier or that you like better. If you do, that's great! It's exactly what the creators of Publisher had in mind when they provided so many alternatives.

A Quick Overview

You don't have to read this book in any particular order. The book is designed so that you can jump in, get the information you need, and then close the book, keeping it near your computer until the next time you need it. But that doesn't mean we scattered the information about with wild abandon. If you were to read the book from front to back, you'd find a logical progression from the simple tasks to the more complex ones. Here's a quick overview.

First, we assume that Publisher 2000 is already installed on your computer. If it's not, the Setup Wizard makes installation so simple that you won't need our help anyway. So, unlike most computer books, this one doesn't start out with installation instructions and a list of system requirements. You've already got that under control.

Sections 2 through 5 of the book cover the basics: starting Publisher; working with menus, toolbars, and dialog boxes; entering text and modifying text; creating text frames; importing text from another file; adjusting character and line spacing; creating bulleted or numbered lists; creating a table of contents; and laying out pages.

Sections 6 through 8 describe tasks for enhancing the look of a publication: inserting objects, clip art, and photographs; layering, aligning, rotating, and flipping objects; working with synchronization; creating and enhancing WordArt; and applying special effects.

Section 9 describes the use of tables to organize information in a publication: creating, resizing, and importing tables; entering text into table cells; inserting and deleting rows and columns; and copying and moving a cell's content.

Section 10 describes ways to work more efficiently using tools that make the creation of repetitive publications quick and easy: using templates; creating personal information sets; and modifying the Design Gallery.

Section 11 describes sharing information between programs for a specific purpose or publication: importing and exporting files; embedding and linking objects; and creating a graph or organization chart.

Section 12 describes tasks to design and create your own Web site: adding hyperlinks or HTML codes; applying color to a Web page; creating a form; saving and previewing Web pages; using a navigation bar; and publishing to the Web.

Section 13 describes ways to add personal information or insert mailing addresses anywhere within the publication to each copy you print: performing mail merges; creating and connecting to a data source; inserting field codes; filtering or sorting a merged publication; and printing a merged publication.

Section 14 describes the final step in the creation of your publication, printing it! There are several ways you can output your finished publication: printing on desktop or color desktop printers; printing envelopes and color separations; creating a postscript file; and preparing a publication for a printing service.

A Final Word (or Two)

We had three goals in writing this book. We want our book to help you:

◆ Do all the things you want to do with Publisher 2000.

◆ Discover how to do things you didn't know you wanted to do with Publisher 2000.

◆ Enjoy doing your work with Publisher 2000.

Our "thank you" for buying this book is the achievement of those goals. We hope you'll have as much fun using *Microsoft Publisher 2000 At a Glance* as we've had writing it. The best way to learn is by doing, and that's what we hope you'll get from this book.

Jump right in!

2

Getting Started with Publisher

When you need to create a great-looking publication, such as a business card, letterhead, newsletter, Web page, or brochure, use Microsoft Publisher 2000 to get the job done quickly and easily.

Introducing Microsoft Publisher

Publisher is a *desktop publishing program*—software you can use to combine text, graphics, and original drawings with sophisticated formatting, all in one easy-to-use package. With Publisher, you can use creative layout and design techniques that were once the exclusive realm of high-priced publishers and graphic designers.

Publisher combines the fundamental power of a word processor and the creativity of a graphics package in a program that is flexible and easy to use. This combination lets you create unique and exciting documents that you could not easily create in any other single application.

Once you have created the publication you want, you can print it on your own printer, package it (electronically) to submit it to a commercial printer, or even publish it on the World Wide Web. In fact, you can do all of these things to the same document.

Starting Publisher

Before you can use Publisher, you need to install it on your computer's hard disk. To work in Publisher, you begin by starting the program. The easiest way to open Publisher is to use the Start button on the Windows taskbar. You can also start Publisher by creating a shortcut on the desktop and then double-clicking the Microsoft Publisher shortcut icon.

TIP

Install features on demand. *Unless you choose the Complete option when installing Publisher, only the most frequently used features are installed. If you attempt to use a feature that is not yet installed, Publisher prompts you to insert the installation disk so that it can install that feature.*

TIP

Don't display the Catalog at startup. *Click the Tools menu, click Options, click the General tab, click to clear the Use Catalog At Start check box, and then click OK.*

Start Publisher

1. Click the Start button on the taskbar.

2. Point to Programs.

3. Click Microsoft Publisher.

The Publisher program window opens and displays the Catalog dialog box. From here you can choose the kind of publication you want to create, or you can open an existing publication.

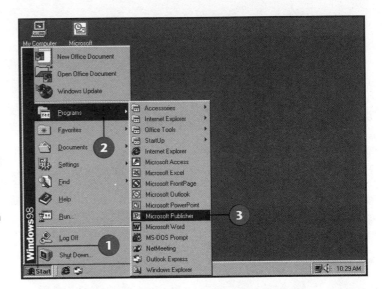

Create a Microsoft Publisher Shortcut

1. Click the Start button on the taskbar, and then point to Programs.

2. Press and hold Ctrl, and then drag the Microsoft Publisher command to the desktop.

A shortcut icon appears.

3. Double-click the shortcut icon.

The Publisher program window opens.

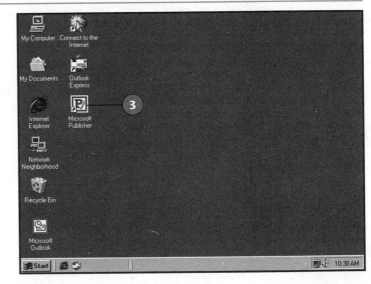

Working with Publisher

Publisher offers many of the text formatting features traditionally associated with word processing software. You can apply fonts and text attributes to design the look you want. You can set tabs, indents, and alignment. Finally, you can edit and correct your text using several handy tools, including design, grammar, and spelling checkers. In addition, you can create tables and merge documents with mailing lists to personalize form letters.

Publisher also lets you work with graphics. Insert graphics (including photos, clip art, and images created in other programs) into your publications. You can also work with easy-to-use tools that allow you create your own graphics.

By far, the most popular and useful tools in Publisher are the wizards. A wizard guides you through the process of completing a task. For example, when you use the Publication Wizard, you answer a few simple questions about your design preferences for your publication and the wizard creates the publication according to your specifications. Then you can use other Publisher tools to add finishing touches. You can preview hundreds of professionally designed publications (invitations, announcements, business cards, newsletters, brochures, awards, and many others), and choose from dozens of creative and coordinated designs. You just select the design elements you want.

Frames and Objects

Each of the elements you work with or create in Publisher is called an *object*. There are text objects for text, picture objects for graphics, draw objects for shapes you create, table objects for tables, and so on. Each object is stored in a *frame*. A frame surrounds an object and allows you to move and size the object in it. As a result, your actions can affect the elements in your publication in two ways. You can make changes to the object itself, such as when you change the font of a text object. And you can change to the object's frame. For example, the background color in the frame can be changed.

You can also use smart objects, which are stored collections of objects. Publisher includes many built-in smart objects for different kinds of common publication elements. For example, a masthead is a built-in smart object that contains text objects, picture objects, and draw objects, all pre-formatted and stored together so that you can insert a masthead quickly into a publication. Of course, you can design and store your own smart objects, (such as a personal logo) to create a library of elements you need for your publications.

2

Viewing the Publisher Window

The title bar displays the name of the publication and the program name.

The menu bar displays the menu items.

Ruler

Toolbars contain frequently used buttons.

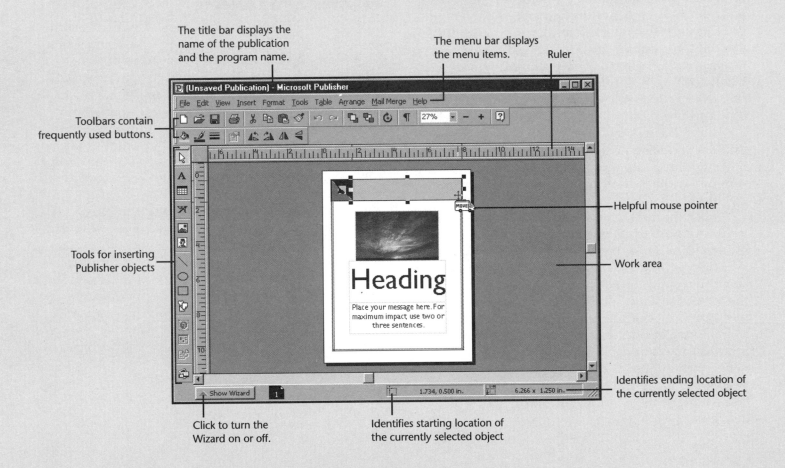

Helpful mouse pointer

Tools for inserting Publisher objects

Work area

Click to turn the Wizard on or off.

Identifies starting location of the currently selected object

Identifies ending location of the currently selected object

Creating a Publication

When you first start Publisher, you see a Catalog dialog box that you can use to create a new publication or open an existing one. You have several options for creating a new publication. You can choose a wizard to help you or you can start from a blank publication. Because you can work on only one publication at a time, Publisher closes the current publication before opening a new one.

TIP

Open an existing publication from the Catalog dialog box. *If you decide to open an existing publication instead of creating a new one, click the Existing Files button to display publications you have already created.*

SEE ALSO

See Section 10, "Creating Custom Publications," on page 155 for information on creating different types of publications.

Create a New Publication

1. Start Publisher. If you have already started Publisher, click the File menu, and then click New.

2. Click the tab to display the method you want to use to create your publication.

3. Click a publication type or design scheme.

4. Click the thumbnail that represents the kind of publication you want to create.

5. If you are using a wizard, click Start Wizard. If you are creating a blank publication, click Create.

6. If you are using a wizard, choose your preferences for the design, color scheme, orientation, logo, printing, and other options. If you are creating a blank publication, begin designing your publication.

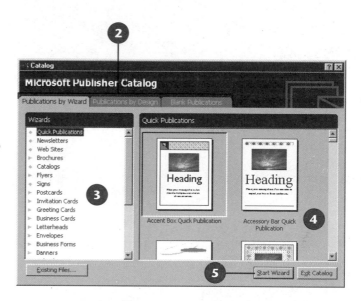

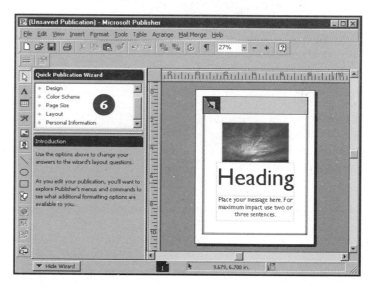

Creating a Blank Publication

Publisher's wizards can be a big help in getting you started when you create a new publication. Every so often, however, you may want to create a unique publication and none of the wizards will do the job. In that case, you can start a blank publication. If you know how to create and use frames, you can create a publication from scratch. Nevertheless, you can still display the wizard in the window to help you think of design elements and options, including orientation and layout. If none of the sample blank publications meet your needs, you can also create a custom page.

Create a Blank Publication

1. Click the File menu, and then click New.

2. Click the Blank Publications tab.

3. Click the kind of publication you want.

4. Double-click the thumbnail that displays the page layout for the publication you want.

   The Publisher window is displayed.

5. Click Design, and then choose a design.

6. Click Color Scheme, and then choose a set of colors.

7. Click Page Size, and then choose the orientation of the page.

8. Click Layout, and then choose the arrangement of text and graphics on the page.

9. Choose the name and address information that you want to appear.

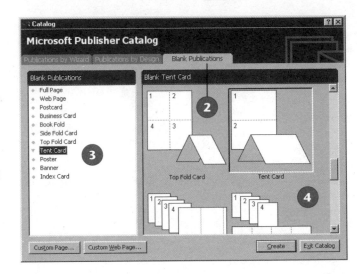

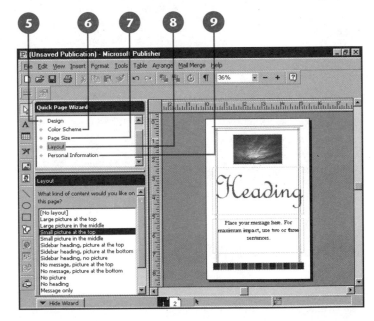

Create a Custom Blank Page

1 Click the File menu, and then click New.

2 Click the Blank Publications tab.

3 Click Custom Page.

4 Choose the layout for the publication.

5 Choose an orientation.

6 Click OK.

No wizard options appear when you create a custom blank publication. Using the Publisher tools, begin designing your publication.

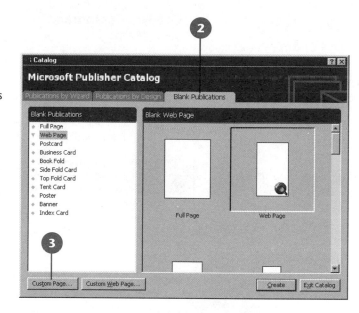

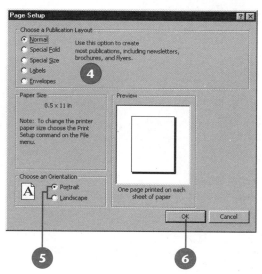

Working with Menus, Toolbars, and Dialog Boxes

In Publisher, you use menus, commands, toolbars, and dialog boxes to carry out tasks. *Menus* are lists of related commands that complete a task. When you first click an item on the menu bar, you see a shorter version of the menu. To see the entire menu, click the arrows at the bottom of the menu list. *Toolbars* contain buttons that carry out a command using default settings and provide a fast way to perform a task. *Dialog boxes* present options for carrying out a command.

Choose a Command on a Menu

1. Click an item on the menu bar.

2. If necessary, click the double arrow to expand the menu and display more commands.

3. If there is an arrow next to a command on the menu, point to the command to see additional related commands.

4. Click the command to choose it or to open a dialog box.

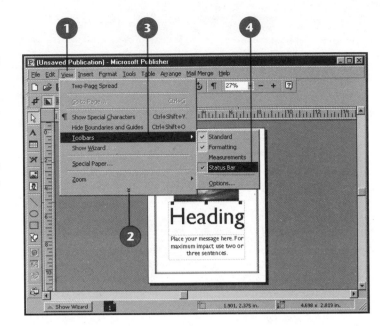

Choose a Command on a Toolbar

1. Click a button on the toolbar.

   You can point to a button for a moment to display the name of the button.

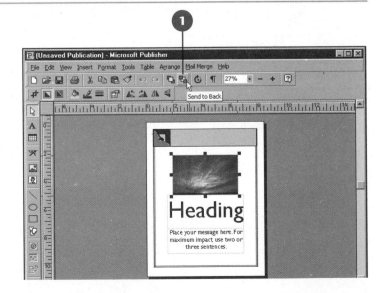

Display a shortcut menu.
When you right-click certain parts of the window or a Publisher object, Publisher displays a short menu of commands that relate only to the item you clicked.

Reset menus. *You can reset the commands on the menus to their original order. Click the Tools menu, click Options, and then click the Reset Usage Data button.*

Personalized toolbars.
When you first open a toolbar, only the buttons you used most recently are visible. Click the More Buttons drop-down arrow to display other toolbar buttons. To display the full toolbar, double-click the gray bar on the left edge of the toolbar.

Display a toolbar button's name. *To find out the name of a toolbar button, position the pointer over the button on the toolbar. The name of the button, or the ScreenTip, appears below the button.*

Choose Dialog Box Options

All Office dialog boxes contain the same types of options, including:

- ◆ Tabs. Click a tab to display its options. Each tab groups a related set of options.

- ◆ Option buttons. Click an option button to select it. You can usually select only one.

- ◆ Spin box. Click the up or down arrow to increase or decrease the number, or type a number in the box.

- ◆ Check box. Click the box to turn the option on or off. A checked box means the option is selected; a cleared box means it's not.

- ◆ List box. Click the drop-down arrow to display a list of options, and then click the option you want.

- ◆ Text box. Click in the box and type the requested information.

- ◆ Button. Click a button to perform a specific action or command. A button name followed by an ellipsis (...) opens another dialog box.

- ◆ Preview box. Many dialog boxes show an image that reflects the options you select.

Tabs Text box

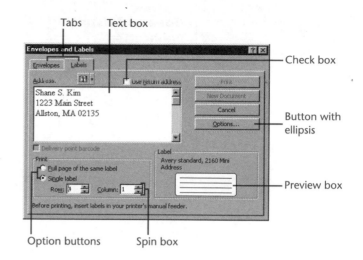

Check box

Button with ellipsis

Preview box

Option buttons Spin box

Confirms your selections and closes the dialog box

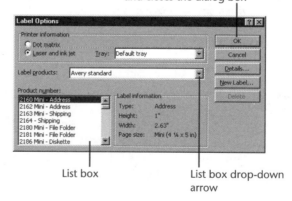

List box List box drop-down arrow

2

Opening a Publication

You can open an existing publication from the program window or the Catalog dialog box. In the program window, use the Open button on the Standard toolbar. In the Catalog dialog box, use the Existing Files button. If you can't recall a file's name or location, use the Find feature in the Open dialog box to locate the file based on the information (or *criteria*) you can recall, such as its creation date, content, author, styles, and so forth.

> **TIP**
>
> **Open a recent file quickly.** *You can open a file on which you recently worked in Publisher by clicking the appropriate filename at the bottom of the File menu.*

> **TIP**
>
> **Delete or rename a file.** *You can delete or rename any closed file from the Open or Save As dialog box. Click the file, click the Tools drop-down arrow, and then click Delete or Rename.*

Open an Existing Publication

1. Click the Open button on the Standard toolbar.

2. Click an icon on the Places bar to open a frequently used folder.

3. If necessary, click the Look In drop-down arrow, and then click the drive where the file is located.

4. Double-click the folder in which the file is stored.

5. Double-click the file you want to open.

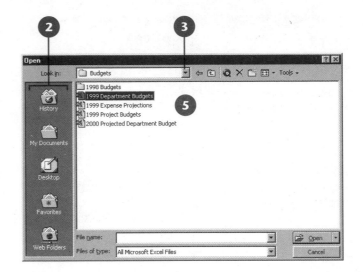

Find a File

1. Click the Open button on the Standard toolbar.

2. Click the Tools drop-down arrow, and then click Find.

3. Click the Look In drop-down arrow, and then click the drive you want to search.

4. Click to select the Search Subfolders check box.

5. Enter as much identifying information as you recall about the file in the Define More Criteria section.

6. Click Find Now.

Identifies information about the file to be found

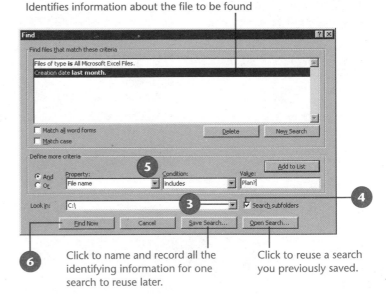

Click to name and record all the identifying information for one search to reuse later.

Click to reuse a search you previously saved.

Selecting Objects

Before you can do anything with an object, you must first select it. Then you can resize or move it with its selection *handles*, the little squares that appear on the edges of the selected object.

TIP

Deselect an object. *Click a blank area in the publication window to deselect a selected object.*

TIP

Use the Tab key to select graphic objects. *If you are having trouble selecting a graphic object that is close to other objects, click a different object and then press Tab until you select the object you want.*

TIP

Select all the objects in a publication quickly. *To select all the objects in a publication, click the Edit menu, and then click Select All.*

Select an Object

1. Click the object you want to select.

   The selection handles that appear around the object indicate that the object is selected.

2. Click another object to deselect a selected object and select the other one.

Selection handles appear on all sides of the selected object.

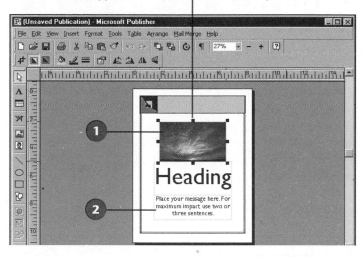

Select Multiple Objects

1. With the Pointer Tool, drag a rectangle to surround the objects you want to select.

   The selection handles that appear around all the objects indicate that they are selected.

2. Press and hold Shift as you click an object to deselect a single object from a group of selected objects.

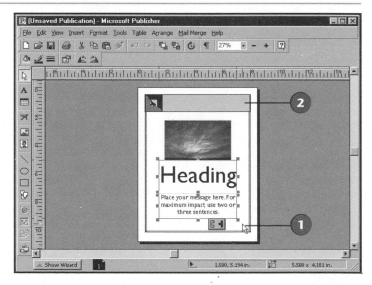

Moving and Resizing Objects

An object (such as text or a graphic) in a publication is like a piece of paper containing text or a picture that you have placed on your page. In the same way you can move a piece of paper, you can rearrange and move objects. Unlike a piece of paper, however, you can also change the size of the object in Publisher.

TIP

Use a corner sizing handle to size proportionally. *To resize without distorting an object's proportions, drag one of the corner sizing handles diagonally.*

TIP

Reverse and redo a change. *To reverse an action, click the Undo button on the Standard toolbar. To repeat an action, click the Redo button on the Standard toolbar.*

Move an Object

1. Select the object you want to move.
2. Place the pointer over the object until the Move pointer appears.
3. Drag the object to a new location.

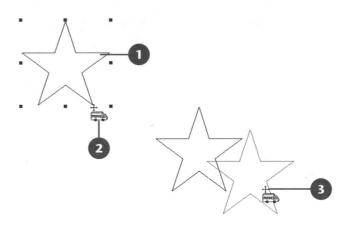

Resize an Object

1. Select the object you want to resize.
2. Place the pointer over a sizing handle until the Resize pointer appears.
3. Drag towards the object's center to reduce the size of the object.
4. Drag away from the object's center to increase the size of the object.

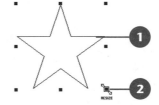 

Cutting, Copying, and Pasting Objects

You can delete, replace, move (*cut*), or *copy* text within one publication or between documents even if they're from different programs. In either case, the steps are the same. If you want to move an object, you can use the Cut feature to remove the object and place it on the *Clipboard*, a temporary storage area. Then you can paste the contents of the Clipboard in a new location.

TIP

Drag to move or copy text.
You can also move or copy selected text without storing it on the Clipboard by using drag-and-drop editing. *To move text, drag the selected text to a new location. To copy text, press and hold Ctrl as you drag the selected text.*

Cut an Object

1. Select an object.

2. Click the Cut button.

   The object is removed from the publication and placed on the Clipboard.

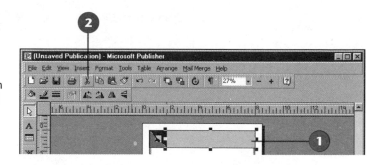

Copy an Object

1. Select the object.

2. Click the Copy button.

   The object remains in the publication and is placed on the Clipboard.

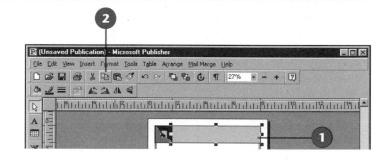

Paste an Object

1. Place the insertion point where you want to insert an object on the Clipboard.

2. Click the Paste button.

   The object is inserted at the insertion point, and remains on the Clipboard.

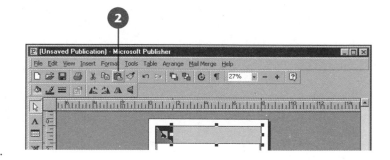

Moving Around in a Publication

Unless you are working in a very small, one-sided publication, such as a business card, you need to move around to see and work in different parts of a publication. You can use the scroll bars to move around on the same page, but to view other pages, you can click the page icons at the bottom of the window. Note that the insertion point does not move as you display different pages. Before you make any changes, click to move the insertion point where you want it on the current page.

TIP

View two pages side by side. *Move to an inside page, click the View menu, and then click Two-Page Spread.*

Move to a Page

1 Click the page icon that corresponds to the page that you want to view.

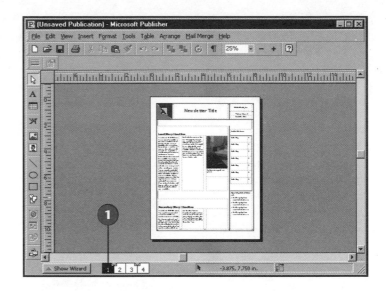

Go to a Page

1 Click the View menu, and then click Go To Page.

The dialog box displays the number of pages in the document.

2 Type the number of the page to which you want to go.

3 Click OK.

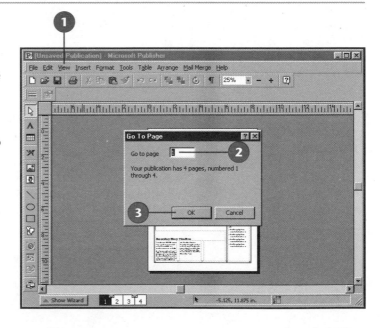

Saving a Publication

Shortly after starting a new publication or making changes to an existing one, you need to permanently store the publication as a file on a disk so you can use it again later. When you save a publication for the first time or save the file with a new name, use the Save As command. When you first save a publication, you give it a name and specify where you want to store it. You can store a publication on your computer's hard disk, or if the publication is smaller than 1.4 megabytes, you can store it on a floppy disk. After you close the publication, you can retrieve it using the name with which you saved it. You can also have Publisher remind you to save your work by setting the AutoSave option.

SEE ALSO

See "Using Templates," on page 164 for information on creating a publication using a template.

Save a New Publication

1. Click the File menu, and then click Save or Save As.

2. Click the Save In drop-down arrow, and then select the location where you want to store the file.

3. Type the name you want to use for the file.

4. If necessary, click the Save As Type drop-down arrow, and then select the type of file you want to save.

5. Click Save.

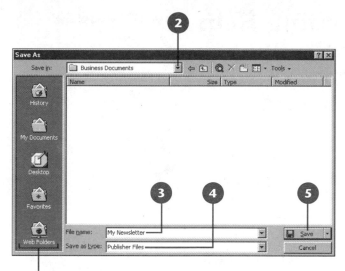

Frequently used folders on the Places bar help you get organized.

Use AutoSave

1. Click the Tools menu, and then click Options.

2. Click the User Assistance tab.

3. Click to select the Remind To Save Publication check box.

4. Enter the amount of time to wait between reminders.

5. Click OK.

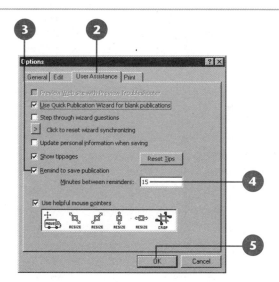

Getting Help from the Office Assistant

Often the easiest way to learn how to accomplish a task is to ask someone who knows. With Office, that knowledgeable friend is always available in the form of the Office Assistant. Tell the Assistant what you want to do in the same everyday language you use to ask a colleague or friend, and the Assistant walks you through the process step by step. If the personality of the default Assistant—Clippit—doesn't appeal to you, choose from a variety of other Assistants.

Ask the Assistant for Help

1. Click the Help button on the Standard toolbar to display the Assistant, or click the Assistant if it is already displayed.

2. Type your question about a task you want help with.

3. Click Search.

4. Click the topic you want help with.

5. Read and follow the directions. After you're done, click the Close button on the Help window.

6. Click the Help button on the Standard toolbar if you want to hide the Assistant.

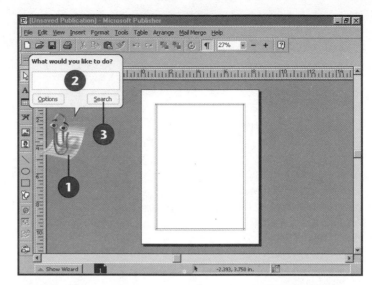

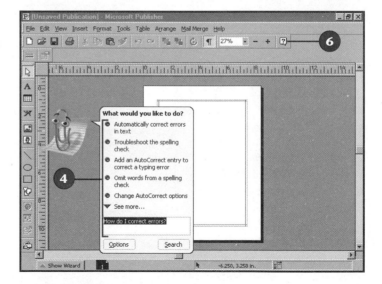

Choose an Assistant

1 Right-click the Assistant and click Options, or click the Options button in the Assistant window.

2 Click the Gallery tab.

3 Click Next and Back to preview different Assistants.

4 Click OK.

If you are prompted, insert the Office 2000 CD-ROM, and then click OK.

The Assistant you want to use is displayed here.

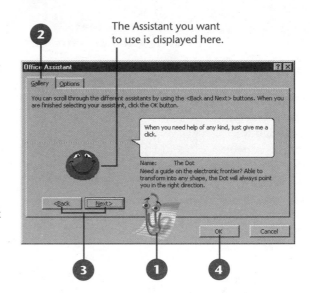

Turn Off the Assistant

1 Right-click the Assistant and click Options, or click the Options button in the Assistant window.

2 Click the Options tab.

3 Click to clear the Use The Office Assistant check box.

4 Click OK.

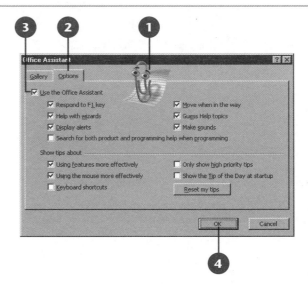

Getting Help by Topic

Publisher provides several ways to get instantaneous help. You can search for information on a particular topic using Publisher's Help topics, or click the Help button on the title bar of a dialog box. Use the Help pointer to get information on any item in the dialog box. If you prefer to use the Help window without the aid of the Office Assistant, you must turn off (not simply hide) the Office Assistant. If you are working with the Office Assistant turned on, you must first enter a question before you can use the Help window.

> **TIP**
>
> **Don't see the Contents, Answer Wizard, and Index tabs?** *Click the Help window title bar to make it active. If you still do not see the tabs, click the Show button on the Help toolbar.*
>
>

Locate Information Using the Contents Tab

1. Click the Help menu, and then click Microsoft Publisher Help.

2. Click the Contents tab.

   This tab displays a table of contents.

3. Click a Help book icon to display a list of topics.

4. Click a topic to open its Help window.

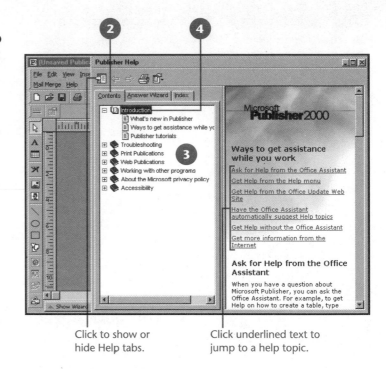

Click to show or hide Help tabs.

Click underlined text to jump to a help topic.

Locate Information Using the AnswerWizard

1. Click the Help menu, and then click Microsoft Publisher Help.

2. Click the Answer Wizard tab.

3. Type a question or topic about which you want information.

4. Click Search.

5. Click a topic.

6. When you're done, click the Close button.

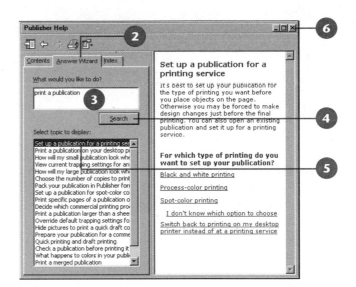

Locate Information Using the Index Tab

1. Click the Help menu, and then click Microsoft Publisher Help.

2. Click the Index tab.

3. Type a topic or click a keyword, and then click Search.

   The index list scrolls to match the letters you type.

4. Click the topic you want.

5. When you're done, click the Close button.

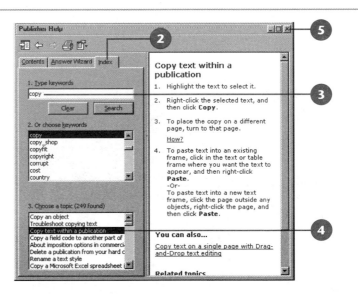

Getting Online Help and Training

Publisher's online tutorials are a series of windows that describe and demonstrate how to use basic, intermediate, and advanced Publisher features. Use tutorials when you want to gain an in-depth understanding of a Publisher concept. Publisher also provides access to help on the Web, available via the Internet. The Microsoft Publisher Web site provides information, tips and tricks, and files, such as sound and video clips.

SEE ALSO

See "Getting Help from the Office Assistant" on page 20 and "Getting Help by Topic" on page 22 for information on getting help on Publisher.

View a Tutorial

1. Click the Help menu, and then click Publisher Tutorials.

2. When the Tutorial window opens, click the topic about which you want to view a tutorial.

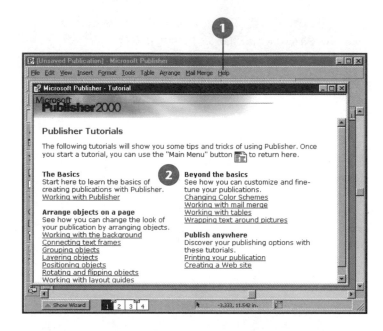

Get Help from Microsoft's World Wide Web Site

1. Make sure you have a modem and Internet access from your computer.

2. Click the Help menu, and then click Microsoft Publisher Web Site.

3. Click the hyperlink for the Microsoft Web site you want.

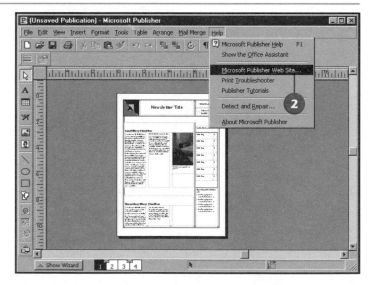

Repairing Publisher Problems

Never again do you need to worry when Publisher stops working for no apparent reason. Publisher is now self-repairing, which means that Publisher checks if essential files are missing or corrupt as a program opens and fixes the files as needed. You may never even realize there was a problem. Other times, Publisher starts fine but might have another problem, such as a corrupted font file or a missing template. These kinds of problems used to take hours to identify and fix. Now Publisher does the work for you with the *Detect And Repair* feature, which locates, diagnoses, and fixes any errors in the program itself. If you need to add or remove features or remove Publisher entirely, you can use Office Setup's maintenance feature.

Detect and Repair Problems

1. Click the Help menu, and then click Detect And Repair.

2. Click Start.

3. Insert the Publisher or Office CD in your CD-ROM drive.

4. If necessary, click Repair Office, and then click the Reinstall Office or Repair Errors In Your Office Installation option button.

5. Click Finish.

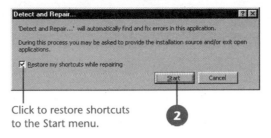

Click to restore shortcuts to the Start menu.

Perform Maintenance on Office Programs

1. In Windows Explorer, double-click the Setup icon on the Publisher or Office CD.

2. Click one of the following maintenance buttons.

   ◆ Repair Office to repair or reinstall Office.

   ◆ Add Or Remove Features to determine which features are installed or removed and when.

   ◆ Remove Office to uninstall Office.

3. Follow the wizard instructions to complete the maintenance.

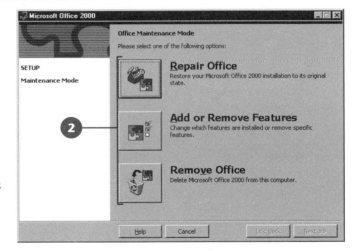

Closing a Publication and Quitting Publisher

After you finish working on a publication, you can close it. Closing a publication makes more computer memory available for other applications. Closing a publication is different from quitting Publisher: after you close a publication, Publisher is still running. When you're finished using Publisher, you can quit the program. To protect your files, always quit Publisher before turning off your computer.

SEE ALSO

See "Saving a Publication" on page 19 for more information about saving your publication.

Close a Publication

1. Click the File menu, and then click Close.

2. If you have made changes to the publication since last saving it, a dialog box opens asking if you want to save changes. Click Yes to save any changes you might have made, or click No to ignore your changes.

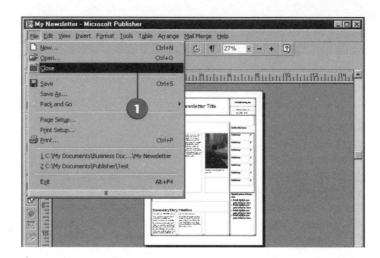

Quit Publisher

1. Click the File menu, and then click Exit, or click the Close button on the Publisher window.

2. If any files are open and you have made any changes since last saving, a dialog box opens asking if you want to save changes. Click Yes to save any changes you've made, or click No to ignore your changes.

You can also click the Close button to exit Publisher and close the publication at the same time.

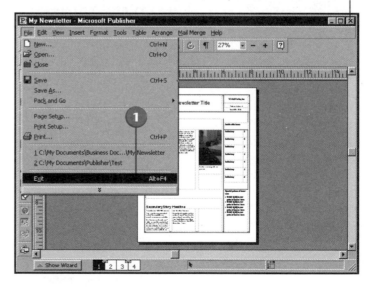

Adding and Editing Text in a Publication

After you create a publication, you can enter and edit text. Text objects are enclosed in a *frame*, which serves as a container to hold a block of text. If you created a publication with a wizard, you see placeholder text, which you replace with your own text in the frame. You can add more text by adding new text frames or by inserting text into an existing text frame. For example, to add a new heading (or some other text) to a brochure, you create a text frame. You create new frames using the corresponding frame tool located on the toolbar at the left side of the window.

After you create a frame, you can move it or change its size to allow for more text (in the case of a text frame). You can enter text by typing it in the frame or you can import text from another file. You can affect the text itself by searching for and replacing text, using hyphenation, and checking the spelling.

If you already know how to use Microsoft Word's text frames, you'll be on familiar ground with Microsoft Publisher 2000 frames. If using frames is new to you, you will still find learning to work with frames a snap.

Creating a Text Frame

When you want to add new text to your publication (rather than edit existing text), you need to create a text frame. Text in a text frame is also called a *text object*. The text in a frame (or in connected frames) is called a *story*. The frame serves as a container in which you can easily format, move, and resize text. Using the Text Frame Tool button (on the Objects toolbar), drag to draw a rectangle that will contain your text. When you release the mouse, the insertion point blinks inside the frame, indicating that you can start typing.

SEE ALSO

See "Entering and Editing Text" on page 29 for information on replacing placeholder text with your own text.

Create a Text Frame

1. Click the Text Frame Tool button on the Objects toolbar.

2. Position the pointer where you want the frame to start, press and hold the mouse button, and drag down and to the right.

3. Release the mouse button when you have created a frame that is the size you want.

The blinking insertion point indicates where text will appear when you begin typing.

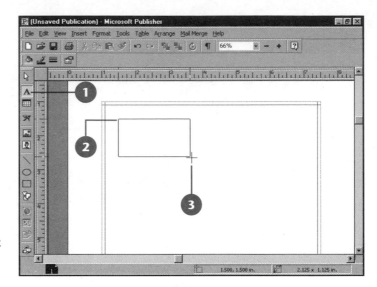

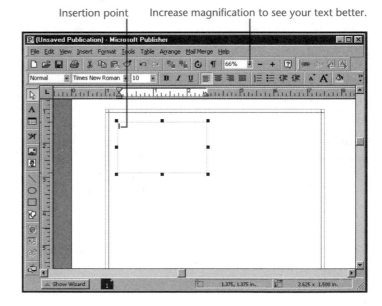

Insertion point   Increase magnification to see your text better.

Entering and Editing Text

When you create a new text frame, the insertion point indicates where text appears when you type. To place the insertion point in your text, move the pointer over the text—the pointer changes to an I-beam to indicate that you can click and then type. If you select text first and then start typing, your new text replaces the selected text. When you create a publication with a wizard, Publisher places generic text in a text frame. The generic text acts as a placeholder. When you click the placeholder, you select all the placeholder text in the frame so that you can easily replace all the text with your own.

TIP

Select all the text in a frame. *To select all the text in a text frame, click the Edit menu, and then click Highlight Entire Story. You can also press Ctrl+A.*

Enter Text into a Frame

1 Click the text frame to select it.

The small boxes on the frame indicate that it is selected.

2 Click the pointer where you want the text to appear.

3 Type the text.

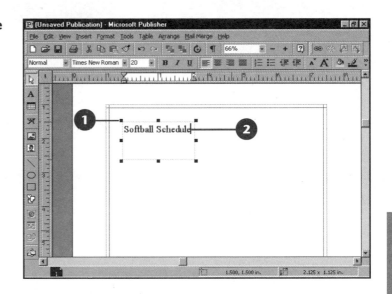

Type Over Existing Text

1 Click the text frame to select it.

2 Drag across the text to select the text you want to replace.

3 Type the text.

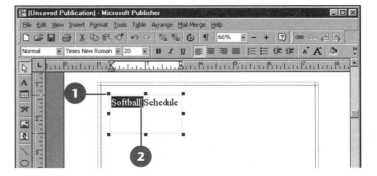

Entering and Editing Text with Microsoft Word

If you prefer to work in Microsoft Word, you can use Word within Publisher to enter and revise the text in a text frame. Publisher opens the Word program window so you can take advantage of Word's tools to edit your text. Note, however, that you cannot insert Word clip art or framed text (text boxes) within a Publisher text frame. You can, however, insert tables you create in Word.

Use Microsoft Word to Insert and Edit Text

1. Right-click text in the text frame.

2. Point to Change Text.

3. Click Edit Story In Microsoft Word on the shortcut menu.

   The Word program window opens.

4. Type the text and edit as necessary using Word's menu commands and toolbar buttons.

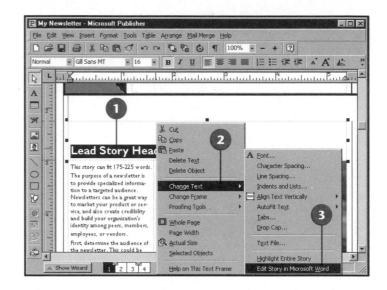

Return to Publisher

1. In Word, click the File menu, and then click Close & Return to [the Publisher document].

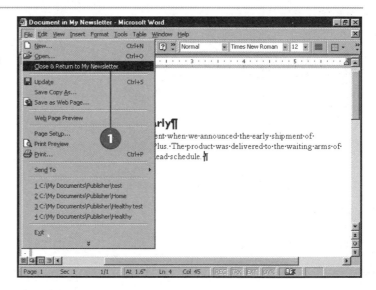

Connecting Frames

If there is more text in a frame than what is currently displayed, you can connect the current frame to another frame. When you connect frames, you identify the empty frame in which you want to "pour" the overflow text (that is, the text that does not fit in the current frame). As you continue to add or remove text in the first frame, Publisher adjusts the amount of text that flows to the connected frame. Connect frames when you do not want to change the size of the text frame to fit the text, or you do not want to adjust the text to fit the frame.

> **TIP**
>
> **Select all the text in a frame.** *To select all the text in a text frame, click the Edit menu, and then click Highlight Entire Story. You can also press Ctrl+ A.*

Connect Text Frames

1. Create an empty text frame.

2. Click to place the insertion point (the text frame that currently contains the excess text).

3. Click the Tools menu, and then click Connect Text Frames.

4. Click the Connect Text Frames button on the toolbar.

    The pointer changes to a cup.

5. Click the empty text frame in which you want the excess text to flow.

This toolbar appears after you choose the Connect Text Frames command.

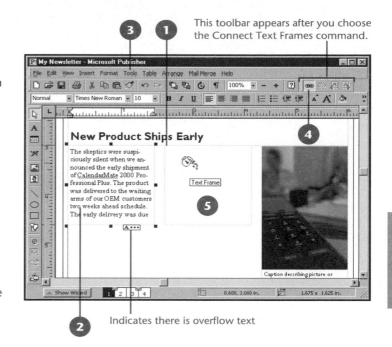

Indicates there is overflow text

Disconnect Text Frames

1. Position the insertion point in the first frame.

2. Click the Disconnect Text Frames button on the toolbar.

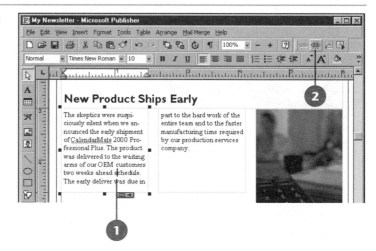

Finding and Replacing Text

When you want to locate words or phrases in a text frame or story, you can use the Find command. If you want to find and then immediately replace the found text with new text, use the Replace command. When you use this command, you can review each occurrence and decide whether to replace the highlighted text. Or you can replace all the occurrences at once, called a *global replace*.

TIP

Search backwards through the document. *If the insertion point is at the end of the story, you can click the Up option button in the Find dialog box to search backwards to the start of the story.*

Find Text

1. Click the Edit menu, and then click Find.

2. Type the text you want to find.

3. Click Find Next.

   The text you searched for is selected.

4. Click Cancel to close the dialog box.

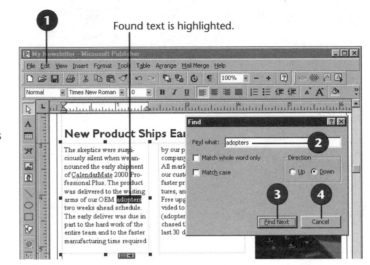

Found text is highlighted.

Replace Each Occurrence of Text

1. Click the Edit menu, and then click Replace.

2. Type the text you want to replace.

3. Type the new text.

4. Click Find Next.

5. Click Replace to replace the selected occurrence.

6. Click Find Next to skip the selected occurrence and locate the next occurrence.

7. Click Close.

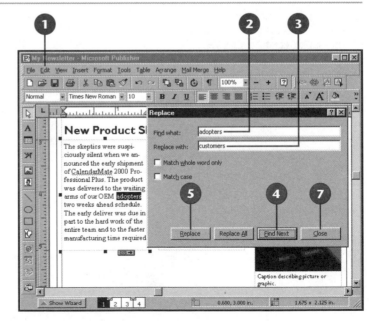

TIP

Match capitalization. *Click to select the Match Case check box in the Find or the Replace dialog box when you want to search for text that matches the capitalization you specify. For example, by searching for only capitalized words, you avoid including those words that do not appear at the start of a sentence.*

TIP

Find only whole words. *To search only for complete words (rather than text that is part of a larger word), click to select the Match Whole Word Only check box in the Find or the Replace dialog box.*

Replace All Occurrences of Text

1 Click the Edit menu, and then click Replace.

2 Type the text you want to replace.

3 Type the new text.

4 Click Replace All.

Publisher displays a message indicating the number of replacements made.

Replaced text

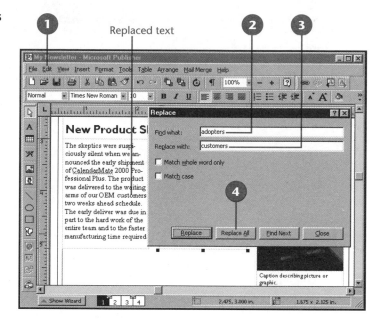

3

FIND AND REPLACE SPECIAL CHARACTERS	
Type this	**To find or replace**
^-	A manual hyphen
^~	A nonbreaking hyphen
^m	All forms of the word
^n	A line break
^ p	A paragraph mark
^s	A nonbreaking space
^t	A tab
^w	Any blank space (spaces and tabs) between characters

Breaking Up Words with Hyphenation

Publisher automatically inserts hyphens to break up words that do not fit at the end of line. This feature actually inserts optional hyphens, meaning that words will be hyphenated only if necessary. If you adjust the width of the line or change the number of words in the line, the hyphen will not appear. To prevent a hyphenated word or phrase from breaking at the end of the line (such as in *part-time*), you can also insert a nonbreaking hyphen. Similarly, you can insert nonbreaking spaces to ensure that a group of words always appears on the same line.

Change Hyphenation Options

1 Click the Tools menu, and then click Options.

2 Click the Edit tab.

3 Click to select the Automatically Hyphenate In New Text Frames check box.

4 Type the distance in which you want words to be hyphenated.

5 Click OK.

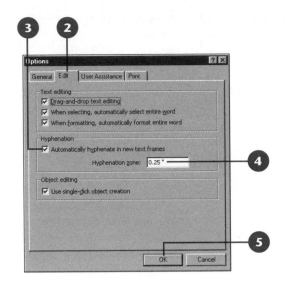

Adjust Hyphenation in a Text Frame

1 Select the text frame in which you want to customize the hyphenation.

2 Click the Tools menu, point to Language, and then click Hyphenation.

3 Click to select the Automatically Hyphenate This Story check box.

4 Adjust the Hyphenation Zone setting.

5 Click OK.

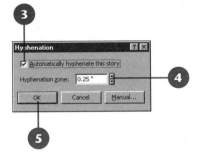

Use Manual Hyphenation

1. Select the text frame in which you want to review the hyphenation.

2. Click the Tools menu, click Language, and then click Hyphenation.

3. Click Manual.

4. Click Yes to accept the new hyphen location, No to reject it, or adjust the position of the hyphen in each occurrence.

5. Click Close.

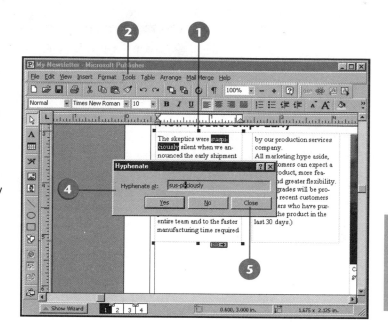

Inserting Symbols

Not all the text you can insert is either a letter or a number. In fact, many symbols are routinely part of a publication. For example, you can insert a degree symbol to indicate the temperature or a section symbol to refer to a specific section of a document. You can choose and insert these symbols from the grid displayed in the Symbol dialog box. You can also insert typographer's symbols such as ™, ©, ®, and an em-dash (—) as you type. As you type certain keystroke combinations, AutoCorrect inserts the symbol.

TIP

Magnify a symbol. *Press and hold the mouse button after you click a symbol to see an enlarged view.*

SEE ALSO

See "Creating AutoCorrect Entries" on page 42 for information on adding and modifying AutoCorrect entries.

Insert a Symbol

1. Place the insertion point where you want to insert a symbol.

2. Click the Insert menu, and then click Symbol.

3. Click the Font drop-down arrow, and then select a font.

4. Click the Subset drop-down arrow, and then select a character group.

5. Click a symbol.

6. Click Insert.

7. When you're done, click Close.

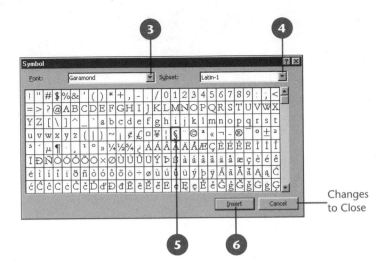

Changes to Close

Insert Symbols as You Type

◆ To replace characters with symbols, two hyphens with an em dash, or straight quotes with smart quotes, continue typing until AutoCorrect makes the appropriate change.

EXAMPLES OF AUTOCORRECT CHANGES		
Type of Correction	**If You Type**	**AutoCorrect Inserts**
Symbols	(tm)	™
Symbols	(c)	©
Symbols	(r)	®
Em dashes	Madison--a small city in southern Wisconsin--is a nice place to live.	Madison—a small city in southern Wisconsin—is a nice place to live.
Smart quotes	" "	" "

Inserting the Date and Time

Your computer always knows the current date and time. You can insert this information in your publication, either as *static text* (text that always remains the same no matter what the date) or as a *field* that is updated every time you open, print, or save the publication.

In the Date And Time dialog box, you can choose from a variety of date and time formats, including European (which displays the day before the month) and military (24-hour) time. You can even specify the language for alternative date formats.

Insert a Date or Time

1 Place the insertion point where you want to insert the date or time.

2 Click the Insert menu, and then click Date And Time.

3 Choose a format from the list.

4 If you want, click the Language drop-down arrow, and then select a language.

5 If you want, click the Update Automatically check box to have the date reflect the current date and time whenever you open, save, or print.

6 Click OK.

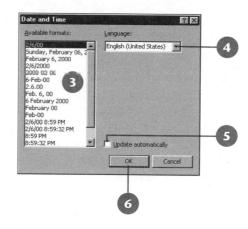

3

Importing Text from Another File

You can save time by importing text you have already created and stored in another program. For example, if you have already developed a promotional letter in Word that contains text you want to use in a brochure, you can bring that text into a text frame in your publication. You can also insert text from files created in Lotus 1-2-3, Word for the Macintosh, and earlier versions of Word. In addition, you can insert text from other Publisher publications.

TIP

Display only the types of files you want to see. *In the Insert Text dialog box, you can locate specific types of files quickly by clicking the Files Of Type drop-down arrow and selecting a file format to display.*

Insert a Text from Another File

1. Place the insertion point where you want to insert text.

   You must be in a text frame before you can insert text from a file.

2. Click the Insert menu, and then click Text File.

3. If necessary, click the Files Of Type drop-down arrow, and then select the format you want to see in the dialog box.

4. Click the file you want to import.

5. Click OK.

   If a specific file type filter was not installed, Publisher will prompt you to insert an installation disk.

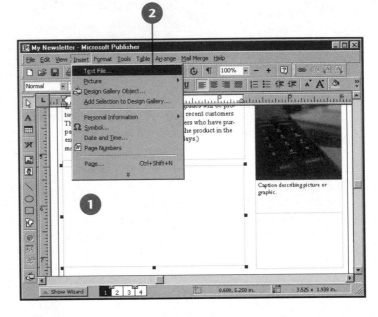

Caption describing picture or graphic.

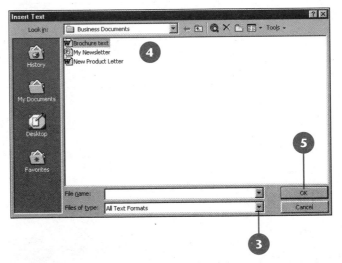

Choosing a Language

When you check the spelling in a publication, words in a foreign language might be identified as misspelled. If you don't want Publisher to identify foreign words as misspelled, you can designate selected text (or all the text in publication) as written in another language. International Microsoft Office users can change the language that appears on their screens by changing the default language settings. Users around the world can enter, display, and edit text in all supported languages, including European languages, Japanese, Chinese, Korean, Hebrew, and Arabic, to name a few.

Choose a Language

1. Select the text to which you want to assign a language.

2. Click the Tools menu, and then click Language.

3. Click Set Language.

4. Click the language you want to mark.

5. If you want, click All Text to set the language for the entire publication.

6. Click OK.

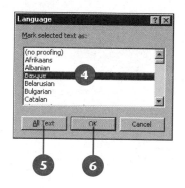

Add a Language to Office Programs

1. Click Start on the Windows taskbar, point to Programs, point to Microsoft Office Tools, and then click Microsoft Office Language Settings.

2. Click to select the check boxes for the languages you want to use.

3. Click OK.

4. Click Yes to quit and restart Publisher.

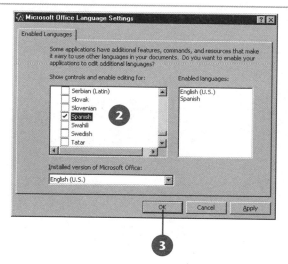

Checking Spelling

Mistakes in a publication can distract your reader from your message, so you want your publication text to be error-free. Publisher provides several tools that help ensure accuracy. You can control spelling errors in a document in three ways:

◆ AutoCorrect replaces common typing errors with the correct spelling as you type. For example, if you type *ahve*, AutoCorrect replaces it with *have*.

◆ You can check the spelling in an entire publication after you've typed it using the Spelling command.

◆ You can set the Spelling feature to alert you to a potentially misspelled word as you type.

Set Spelling Options

(1) Click the Tools menu, click Spelling, and then click Spelling Options.

(2) Click to select the check boxes of the spelling features you want.

(3) Click OK.

Check Spelling

(1) Click the Spelling button on the Standard toolbar.

(2) If the Spelling dialog box opens,

◆ Click Ignore if the word is spelled correctly.

◆ Click the correct spelling, and then click Change.

◆ Click Delete if the error is a repeated word.

(3) Click OK when a message box tells you the spelling check is complete.

You can type your correction here.

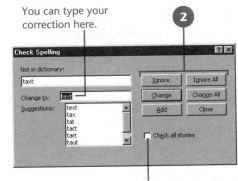

Click to check all the text in the publication.

Identify Spelling Errors as You Type

1. Right-click any word that is underlined with a red wavy line.

2. Click a suggested spelling on the shortcut menu.

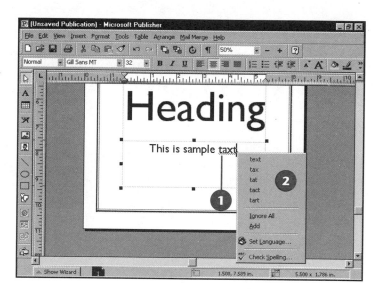

3

Creating AutoCorrect Entries

Publisher includes many AutoCorrect entries that correct commonly misspelled words as you type. However, you can also use AutoCorrect to create entries that are abbreviations for longer words or expressions. That way, when you type an abbreviation, Publisher inserts the longer word or phrase. This feature saves you time and prevents errors. Of course, you can always create entries for words you often misspell that are not already included in Publisher's AutoCorrect list.

Set AutoCorrect Options

1 Click the Tools menu, and then click AutoCorrect.

2 Click the AutoCorrect tab.

3 Click to select the check boxes of the features you want or click to clear the check boxes for the features you do not want.

4 Click OK.

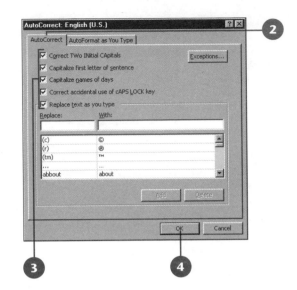

Create an AutoCorrect Entry

1 Click the Tools menu, and then click AutoCorrect.

2 Click the AutoCorrect tab.

3 Type the abbreviation or name of the new entry. This is the text that you will type.

4 Type the text of the entry. This is the text that will be inserted.

5 Click Add.

6 Click OK.

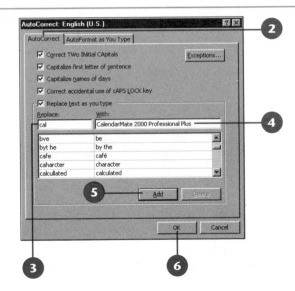

Insert an AutoCorrect Entry

1. Place the insertion point where you want to insert an AutoCorrect entry.

2. Type the AutoCorrect entry name.

   After you press the Spacebar, Publisher inserts the assigned AutoCorrect text.

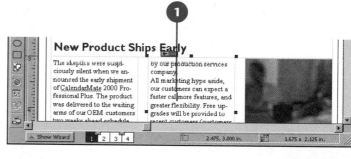

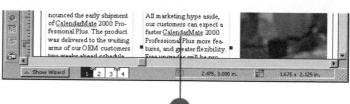

Delete an AutoCorrect Entry

1. Click the Tools menu, and then click AutoCorrect.

2. Click the AutoCorrect tab.

3. Click to select the entry you want to delete.

4. Click Delete.

5. Click OK.

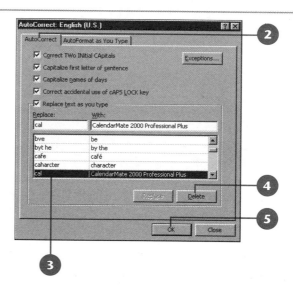

Specifying Editing Options

Publisher includes plenty of editing features that make it easy to use. These features are turned on by default. If you try to use a particular feature, but find it is not enabled, display the Edit tab in the Options dialog box (click the Tools menu, and then click Options). Check the feature you want to use. If, on the other hand, you prefer to work without certain editing features, you can turn them off.

Allows you to copy and move text by selecting and dragging it to a new location

Selects an entire word as you highlight text to select it

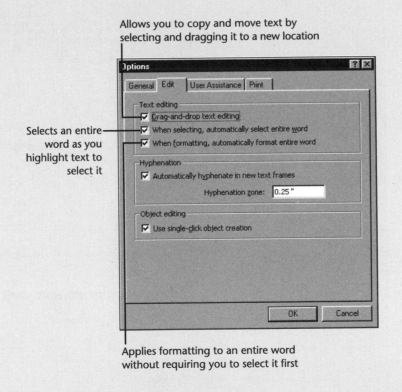

Applies formatting to an entire word without requiring you to select it first

4

Changing the Appearance of Text

Once you have entered text into your publication, you can improve the appearance of the text (and the publication as a whole) by formatting the text. There are many ways to format text, including changing the appearance of the characters, changing the alignment and line spacing of paragraphs, and adding borders and backgrounds to the text frame.

You can change the appearance of characters by changing the font (also known as the typeface) and the font size. You can also apply font effects such as bold, italics, and outline, among others. You can even change the color of text, and stretch and condense text.

You can align a paragraph by changing its position (such as right-aligned or centered) relative to the text frame. You can align columns of text (including numbers) using tabs. If your text frame contains a list of items, you might start each item with a bullet or number. Indenting and changing the space between lines are other ways to format a paragraph. In addition, you can add a background and border to the text by applying these features to the text frame itself. To save time, you can store collections of formatting in styles, and then apply styles to quickly format text consistently. You can also copy formatting to other text using the Format Painter feature.

Changing the Font and Size of Text

A *font* is set of characters (letters, numbers, symbols, and punctuation), all of a particular design or typeface. Fonts such as Arial or Times New Roman are suitable for no-nonsense business documents. Other fonts such as Zapf Chancery or Brushscript are better suited to special documents such as wedding invitations or announcements. When choosing a font, consider the tone and audience for your publication and be sure to choose a font that is consistent with the impression you want to make. Take care to limit the number of decorative fonts you use. No matter what font you use, you can also change its size. A font size is measured in *points* (abbreviated pts), which is 1/72 of an inch.

Change the Font

1. Select the text you want to format.

2. Click the Font drop-down arrow on the Formatting toolbar.

3. Click the font you want to apply to your text.

   If no text was selected, the new font is applied to the word next to the pointer.

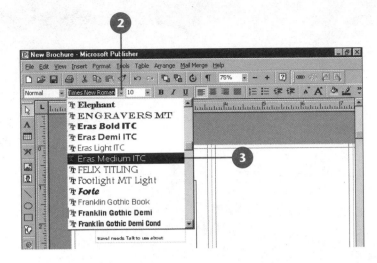

Change the Font Size

1. Select the text you want to format.

2. Click the Font Size drop-down arrow on the Formatting toolbar.

3. Click the point size you want to apply to your text.

Click to decrease the font size.

Click to increase the font size.

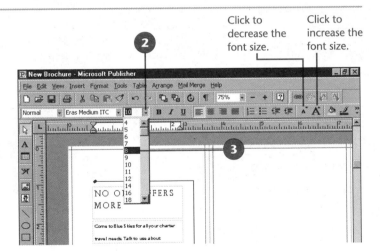

Changing Font Effects

You can further change the appearance of text by applying special effects. For example, you can format text in bold, italics, or underlining, apply a new color, or use any combination of these settings. These frequently used effects are available with the click of a button on the Formatting toolbar. In the Font dialog box, you can apply any of the following effects:

◆ Superscript or subscript

◆ Outline, emboss, shadow, or engrave

◆ Small caps or all caps

Apply Bold, Italics, or Underlining to Text

1 Select the text you want to format.

2 Click the button on the Formatting toolbar you want to apply.

You can click the button again to turn off the feature.

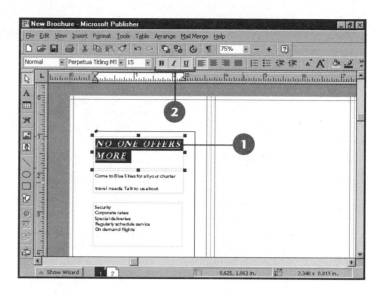

Apply a Font Effect

1 Select the text you want to format.

2 Click the Format menu, and then click Font.

3 Click the effect you want to apply.

4 Click Apply to apply these changes but leave the dialog box open so you can make additional changes.

5 Click OK.

Click to choose underlining options.

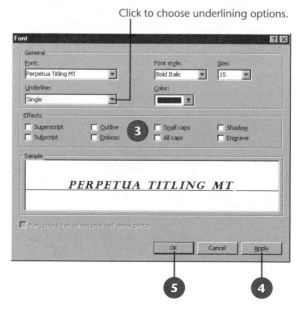

Adjusting Character Spacing

When you are working with a very large font size, you can improve the appearance of the text by decreasing the spaces between characters. In addition, you can achieve a creative effect by increasing the spaces between characters, as in a small font that is part of a logo. You can also adjust the space between two individual characters (called *kerning*) or between all the characters in a selected block of text (called *tracking*). In addition, you can stretch or shrink the width of the characters themselves. By default, Publisher adjusts the kerning for pairs of text larger than 14 points, but you can change the font size at which you want automatic kerning to begin, or you can turn off automatic kerning entirely.

Stretch or Shrink Characters

1. Select the text you want to format.

2. Click the Format menu, and then click Character Spacing.

3. Click the Scaling up arrow to stretch the width of the characters, or down arrow to shrink the width of selected characters.

4. Click OK to accept these settings, or click Apply to apply these changes but leave the dialog box open.

Adjust Space Between Selected Characters

1. Select the text you want to format.

2. Click the Format menu, and then click Character Spacing.

3. Click the Tracking drop-down arrow, and then select a preset tracking setting.

4. Click OK to accept these settings, or click Apply to apply these changes but leave the dialog box open.

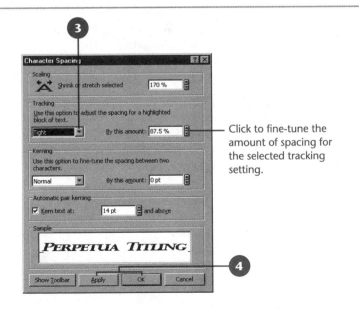

Click to fine-tune the amount of spacing for the selected tracking setting.

Kern common characters.
Consider kerning after uppercase characters (particularly after the letters "P" "T" and "W").

Kern automatically when you are working with a large font. *In the Character Spacing dialog box, click to select the Kern Text At check box, and then enter the font size at which you want to turn on automatic kerning.*

Adjust Kerning Between Character Pairs

1. Place the insertion point between the characters for which you want to adjust the kerning.

2. Click the Format menu, and then click Character Spacing.

3. Click the Kerning drop-down arrow, and then select a preset kerning setting.

4. If you want, click the By This Amount up arrow to increase or down arrow to decrease the space between selected characters.

5. Click OK.

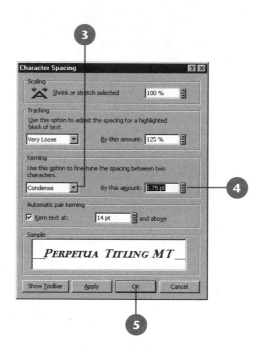

Changing Paragraph Alignment

Aligning paragraphs determines the appearance of the left and right edges of text within a text frame. For example, center alignment evenly positions text between the left and right edges of the frame, while justified alignment adjusts the space between words to create even left and right edges. You can also indent text from either or both edges of the frame, and use preset indent options to create the look you want. To align text between the page margins, you need to extend the text frame all the way to the margins.

Change Paragraph Alignment

1. Select the text you want to align, or click the text frame to align the text within it.

2. Click the corresponding alignment button on the Formatting toolbar.

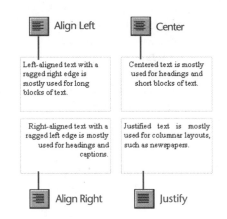

Align Left

Left-aligned text with a ragged right edge is mostly used for long blocks of text.

Center

Centered text is mostly used for headings and short blocks of text.

Right-aligned text with a ragged left edge is mostly used for headings and captions.

Justified text is mostly used for columnar layouts, such as newspapers.

Align Right

Justify

Change Indentation

1. Select the text you want to indent.

2. Click the Format menu, and then click Indents And Lists.

3. Click the Normal option button.

4. Click the Preset drop-down arrow, and then select the indent option you want.

5. If you want, enter the distances you want to indent the text in the appropriate text boxes.

6. Click OK.

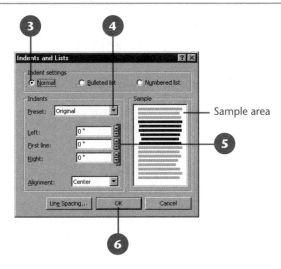

Sample area

TIP

Indent text quickly. *With the insertion point in the paragraph you want to indent, click the Increase Indent or the Decrease Indent button on the Formatting toolbar. Each time you click, you increase or decrease the indentation one half inch.*

SEE ALSO

See "Creating AutoCorrect Entries" on page 42 for information on adding and modifying AutoCorrect entries.

SEE ALSO

See "Creating Bulleted Lists" on page 54 and Creating Numbered Lists" on page 56 for information on creating and modifying bulleted and numbered lists.

Create a Hanging Indent

1. Select the text you want to indent.

2. Click the Format menu, and then click Indents And Lists.

3. Click the Normal option button.

4. Click the Preset drop-down arrow, and then click Hanging Indent.

5. Click OK.

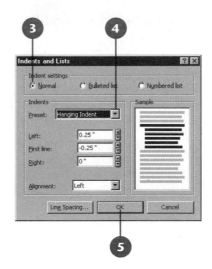

4

Displaying Rulers

To make it easier for you to align and position text on the page, you can use the horizontal and vertical rulers. By default, the horizontal ruler appears at the top of the window, and the vertical ruler appears at the left edge of the window. However, you can move the rulers closer to the area where you want to work. You can also hide the rulers entirely if you want more space in the window for your publication.

SEE ALSO

See "Setting Up Layout Guides" on page 72 for information on using rulers with layout and grid guides.

Turn Rulers On and Off

1 Click the View menu.

2 Click Rulers.

When a check mark appears next to the Rulers command, rulers are turned on. When no check mark appears, rulers are turned off.

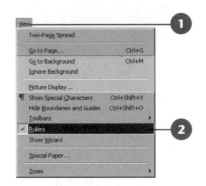

Move Rulers

1 Position the pointer in the upper-left corner of the ruler, and then drag the pointer:

- ◆ Down to move the horizontal ruler.

- ◆ To the right to move the vertical ruler.

- ◆ Diagonally to move both rulers at the same time.

Drag diagonally to move both rulers.

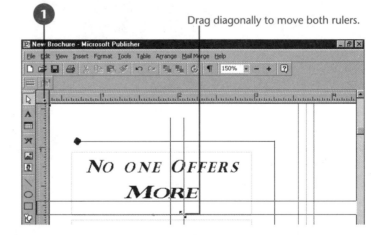

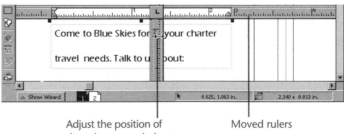

Adjust the position of the ruler as needed.

Moved rulers

Aligning Text with Tabs

Aligning text with tabs is a convenient way to place text at opposite ends of a text frame or to create a simple table of numbers. A *tab* or *tab stop* is a character you use to align text to a specific location in the text frame. When you press the Tab key, the text after the tab character moves to the next tab position. Default tab stops are located every half inch, but you can create tab stops (with left, right, center, and decimal alignment) to align text where you want. You can use the ruler to create tab stops or you can use the Tabs dialog box to create *leader tabs* (tab stops with a line or row of dots, dashes, or bullets in front of the tabbed text).

Set a Tab Stop

1 Place the insertion point in the paragraph you want to format with a tab.

2 Click the Tab Alignment button until the icon for the alignment you want appears.

3 Click on the ruler where you want to set the tab stop.

You can reposition the tab stop by dragging it to a new location.

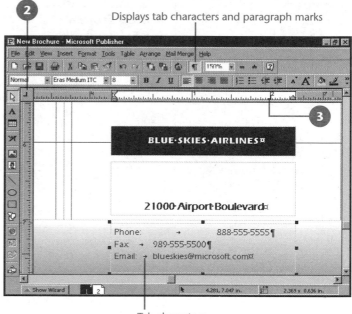

Displays tab characters and paragraph marks

Tab characters

Create a Leader Tab Stop

1 Click the Format menu, and then click Tabs.

2 Type the tab position.

3 Click an alignment option button.

4 Click a Leader option button.

5 Click Set.

6 Click OK.

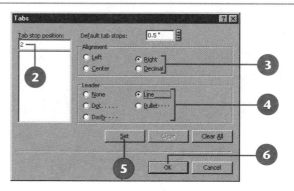

4

Creating Bulleted Lists

A *bullet* is a small symbol or graphic that appears in front of each item in a list. Formatting a list with bullets helps your reader quickly identify the listed items. When you create a new line in a list, Publisher automatically places a bullet and a tab character at the start of the new line. You can customize the appearance of your bullets by changing the bullet symbol and the size of the bullet. Each item in a list is formatted as a paragraph with a hanging indent.

TIP
Turn off bullets at the end of a list. *Press Enter twice after typing the last item in a list.*

TIP
Create a bulleted list from scratch. *Create a text frame, click the Bullets button on the Formatting toolbar, and then start typing.*

Create or Remove Bullets from a List for Existing Text

1 Select the text you want to format with bullets or the list from which you want to remove bullets.

2 Click the Bullets button on the Formatting toolbar.

Bullets

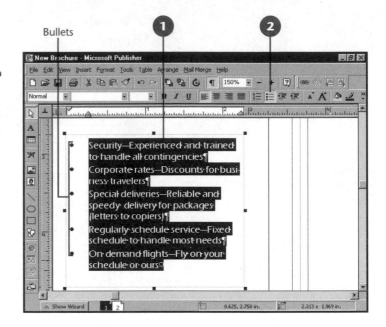

Change the Bullet Type

1. Select the bulleted list.

2. Click the Format menu, and then click Indents And Lists.

3. Click a new bullet type.

4. If you want, click New Bullet to select a new bullet that is not currently displayed.

5. Click a symbol that you want to use.

6. Click Insert.

7. Click the Size up or down arrows to increase or decrease the size of the bullet.

8. Click the Indent List By up or down arrows to increase or decrease the amount the list is indented from the bullet.

9. Click the Alignment drop-down arrow, and then select the alignment you want.

10. Click OK.

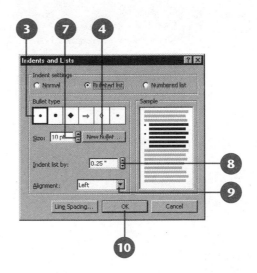

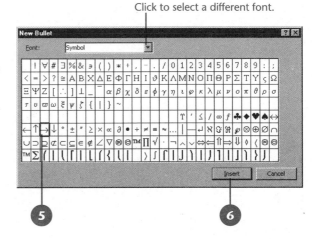

Click to select a different font.

4

Creating Numbered Lists

When you want to reinforce the idea of a sequence or priority in a list, you can create a numbered list. When you create a new line in a numbered list, Publisher places the next number (and a tab character) at the start of the new line. If you delete or insert a line in the middle of a list, Publisher automatically renumbers the remaining items. By default, Publisher numbers the list with Arabic numerals followed by a period (1., 2., 3., and so on), but you can change the format of the numbers to letters (A., B., C...., or a., b., c....). You can also change or delete the character that follows the number. Each item in a numbered list is formatted as a hanging indented paragraph, but you can change how much the list is indented.

Create or Remove Numbers from a List for Existing Text

1 Select the text you want to format with numbers or the list from which you want to remove numbers.

2 Click the Numbering button on the Formatting toolbar.

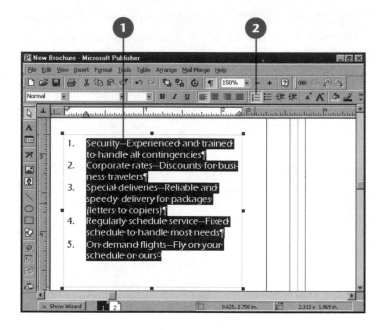

Change the Number Format

1. Select the numbered list.

2. Click the Format menu, and then click Indents And Lists.

3. Click the Format drop-down arrow, and then click a number format.

4. Click the Separator drop-down arrow, and then click a separator character.

5. Click the Start At up or down arrows to specify a new number with which to start numbering.

6. Click the Indent List By up or down arrows to increase or decrease the amount the list is indented from the numbers.

7. Click the Alignment drop-down arrow to change the alignment of the list.

8. Click OK.

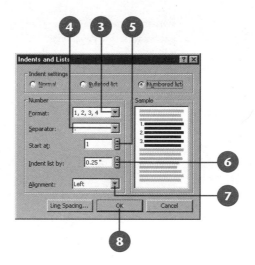

4

Adjusting Line Spacing

You can adjust the amount of space between the lines in a paragraph to create a more "open" look to your publication. You can also change the amount of space before and after individual paragraphs. Using the Line Spacing feature to adjust spacing gives you greater control and precision than simply pressing Enter to create blank space between lines of text. The space between lines within a paragraph is measured by the height of one line. The space between paragraphs is measured in points.

TRY THIS

Adjust the spacing before and after paragraphs in lists. *In the Indents And Lists dialog box, click the Line Spacing button to open the Line Spacing dialog box, and then adjust the space before and after the items in a list.*

Change Spacing within a Paragraph

1. Place the insertion point in the paragraph you want to format.

2. Click the Format menu, and then click Line Spacing.

3. Click the Between Lines up or down arrows to increase or decrease the amount of space between lines in your publication.

4. Click OK.

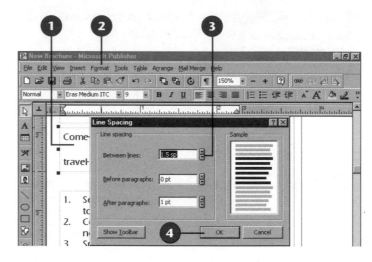

Change Spacing Between Paragraphs

1. Place the insertion point in the paragraph you want to format.

2. Click the Format menu, and then click Line Spacing.

3. Click the Before Paragraphs up or down arrows to increase or decrease the amount of space before paragraphs.

4. Click the After Paragraphs up or down arrows to increase or decrease the amount of space after paragraphs.

5. Click OK.

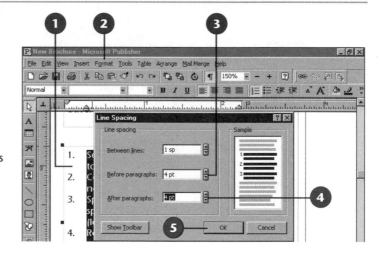

Copying Formatting

If you have applied a number of formatting settings that you want to apply to other text in the publication, using the Format Painter to copy the formatting is a fast way to apply multiple formatting settings to text throughout the publication.

TIP

Leave the Format Painter turned on after each use.
Double-click the Format Painter button after selecting the formatting you want to copy. Click the Format Painter button again or pres Esc to turn off the Format Painter.

SEE ALSO

See "Creating a Consistent Look" on page 62 for information on using styles.

Copy Formatting

1 Select the text whose formatting you want to copy.

Select the paragraph mark if you want to copy paragraph formatting.

2 Click the Format Painter button on the Standard toolbar.

3 Drag the Format Painter pointer across the text you want to format.

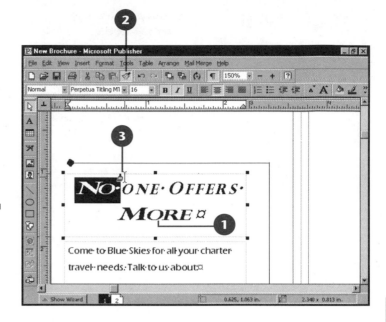

Creating a Dropped Capital Letter

One way to achieve a formal and creative look in a publication is to use a dropped capital letter at the start of a paragraph. Also known as a *drop cap*, this formatting allows the first letter in a paragraph to be dramatically larger than the surrounding text. Depending on the option you choose the font of the drop cap may also change. You can create a dropped capital letter quickly in Publisher with the Drop Cap command. You can choose from several preset formats or you can customize the formatting of the drop cap to fit your needs.

Create a Dropped Capital Letter

1 Place the insertion point in the paragraph in which you want to create a dropped capital letter.

2 Click the Format menu, and then click Drop Cap.

3 Scroll through the available preset drop cap options and click the one you want.

4 Click Apply to apply these changes but leave the dialog box open, or click OK to apply and close the dialog box.

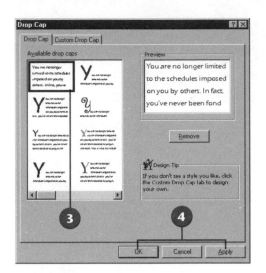

Remove a Dropped Capital Letter

1 Place the insertion point in the paragraph from which you want to remove a dropped capital letter.

2 Click the Format menu, and then click Drop Cap.

3 Click Remove.

4 Click OK.

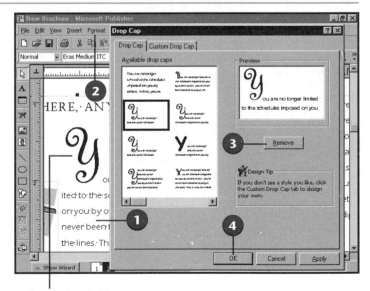

Dropped capital letter

TIP

Use decorative or ornate fonts. *If the surrounding text is rather simple, use a contrasting, exciting font for the dropped capital letter.*

SEE ALSO

See "Adjusting Character Spacing" on page 48 for information on kerning and tracking text.

Customize a Dropped Capital Letter

1. Place the insertion point in the paragraph in which you want to customize a dropped capital letter.

2. Click the Format menu, and then click Drop Cap.

3. Click the Custom Drop Cap tab.

4. Click the position for the drop cap.

5. Click the Lines up or down arrows to adjust the position of the drop cap.

6. Click the Size Of Letters up or down arrows to adjust the height of the drop cap.

7. Click the Number Of Letters up or down arrows to specify the number of letters to be formatted as a drop cap.

8. Click the Font drop-down arrow, and then select a font.

9. Click the Font Style drop-down arrow, and then select a font style.

10. Click the Color drop-down arrow, and then select a color.

11. Click OK.

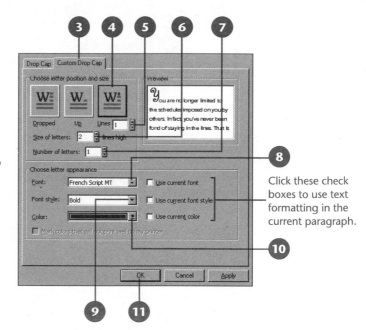

Click these check boxes to use text formatting in the current paragraph.

Creating a Consistent Look

When you create a collection of related publications, such as those for a specific event or organization, make sure that all the publications look similar. By using consistent choices of colors, design elements, and text formatting, your readers will instantly recognize that all your publications are related to the same effort or company. Publisher's Catalog and color schemes can help you achieve consistent designs and colors. Use *text styles*, which store text formatting settings, to ensure your text formatting is consistent in all your publications. After creating a text style in a publication, you can import or export the style to other publications.

SEE ALSO

See "Copying Formatting" on page 59 for information on using the Format Painter to create a consistent look.

Create a New Text Style

1. If you want, select the text from which you want to base a new style.

2. Click the Format menu, and then click Text Styles.

3. Click Create A New Style.

4. Enter a name for the new style.

   At first, the new style's settings are the same as the settings in the selected text.

5. Click each of the formatting options and change the formatting settings for the new style.

6. Click Close.

7. Click OK.

   You can now apply the style to selected text.

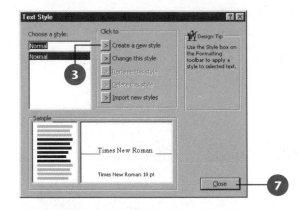

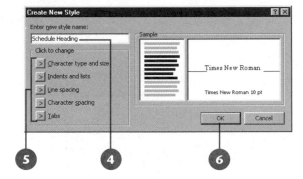

Apply a Text Style

1. Click the text frame to select it.

2. Click the Style drop-down arrow on the Formatting toolbar.

3. Choose the text style you want to apply.

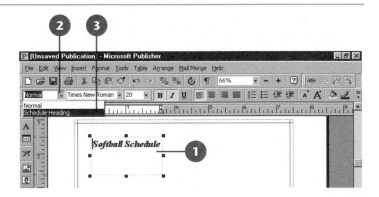

Import a Style

1 Click the Format menu, and then click Text Style.

2 Click Import New Styles.

3 Double-click the publication that contains the styles you want to import.

4 Click Close.

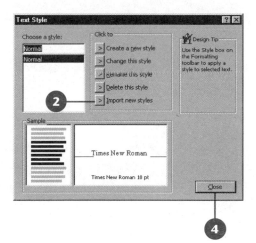

Change a Style

1 Select the text whose style you want to change.

2 Click the Format menu, and then click Text Styles.

3 Click Change This Style.

4 Click each of the formatting options and change the formatting settings for the new style.

5 Click OK.

6 Click OK.

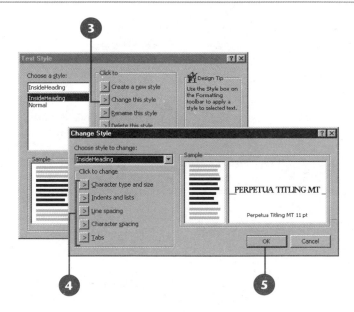

4

Adding Background Color to Text

You can add a color background to text by filling the text frame with a color or pattern. There are three types of color backgrounds you can create:

◆ Use a solid color to draw your reader's attention to a specific area.

◆ Use a gradient fill (where a color fades from lighter to darker) to create a feeling of movement or to add dimension.

◆ Use patterns to give texture to your publication.

TRY THIS

Apply a patterned background. *In the Fill Effects dialog box, click the Patterns option button. Scroll to review different patterns, and then click the one you want.*

Add a Background Color

1. Click the text frame to which you want to add a background color.

2. Click the Fill Color button on the Formatting toolbar.

3. Click the color you want.

4. If you want, click More Colors to view additional color options. Click the color you want, and then click OK.

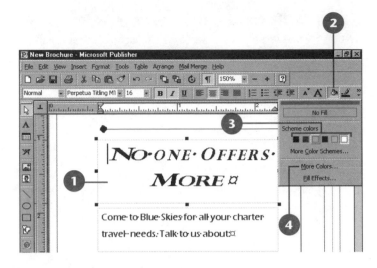

Add a Gradient Fill Background

1. Click the text frame to which you want to add a gradient fill background.

2. Click the Fill Color button on the Formatting toolbar.

3. Click Fill Effects.

4. Click the fill effect you want.

5. Click the Base Color drop-down arrow, and then select a base color.

6. Click the Color 2 drop-down arrow, and then select a second color.

7. Click OK.

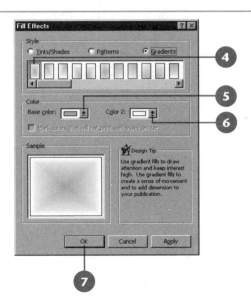

Adding a Border Around Text

You can add a border to a text frame to draw attention to important information. In addition, you can apply a color to your border. You can also change the line style of the border by choosing multiple lines and line thicknesses. Remember to apply these options carefully. Too much formatting can be distracting.

SEE ALSO

See "Drawing a Line or Border" on page 94 and "Working with BorderArt" on page 96 for information adding lines and borders to your publication.

Add or Change a Border

1. Click the text frame to which you want to add or change a border.

2. Click the Line/Border Style button on the Formatting toolbar.

3. Click the line style you want.

4. If you want, click More Styles. Click the border you want, and then click OK.

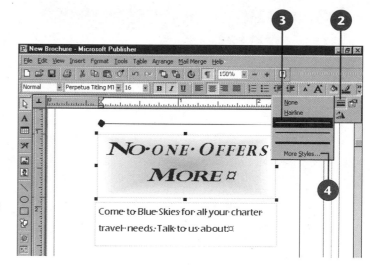

Change the Line Color

1. Click the text frame in which you want to change the border line color.

2. Click the Line Color button on the Formatting toolbar.

3. Click the color you want.

4. If you want, click More Colors. Click the color you want, and then click OK.

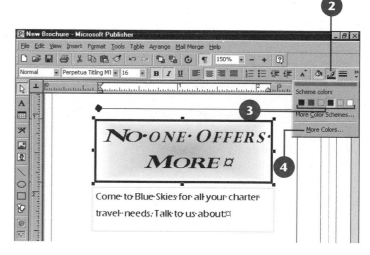

Changing AutoFormat Options

Some formatting in Publisher takes place automatically. For example, when you type an asterisk followed by a tab in front of a paragraph, Publisher will automatically convert the asterisk to a bullet. When you press Enter at the end of the line, Publisher will display another bullet so that you create a bulleted list. Similarly, you can automatically create numbered lists by beginning a new line with a number and tab. Publisher converts dashes and double dashes to en and em dashes respectively. You can turn off the AutoFormat option for each of these features if you prefer to have more control over the formatting as you type.

Change AutoFormat Options

1. Click the Tools menu, and then click AutoCorrect.

2. Click the AutoFormat As You Type tab.

3. Click to clear the options that you want to turn on or off.

4. Click OK.

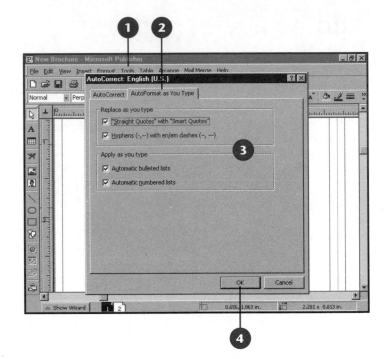

5

Laying Out Pages

After you create a publication, you can make it more appealing by fine-tuning its layout. Each publication is different and can have unique settings that used to be available only to high-priced design firms.

Using Professional Layout Tools

A publication has controls that determine its margins and boundaries. Within a publication are many elements, such as text frames and graphic images, that may have their own margins. Each publication has its controls for margins, called layout guides, and several options for units of measurement. You can also change the type and size of paper on which you print, the orientation of the printed material, and how and where page numbers are printed.

Microsoft Publisher 2000 has a variety of tools that make it easy for you to produce professional publications. These tools let you align text and control how it fits within a frame. Publisher makes it easy to create notices that tell readers where related story text can be found, and automatically updates them when you move a frame or add or remove pages. To make it easy for readers to find specific topics in a publication, the Design Gallery includes many different styles of tables of contents that you can insert directly into your publication.

Inserting and Removing Pages

Once you've created your publication, you may find you need to add or remove pages. Publisher makes it easy to insert or delete pages. If you are working on a newsletter that has pages with left- and right-hand layouts, add or delete pages in multiples of two, because inserting or removing an odd number of pages would ruin the remaining layout. The view you're in determines the default number of pages to add or delete. So, if you're viewing a publication in Two-Page Spread view, the default will be 2 when you give the command to add or remove pages.

SEE ALSO

See "Setting Up Layout Guides" on page 72 for information on creating mirrored pages.

Add a Page

(1) Click the page after which the new page(s) will be added.

(2) Click the Insert menu, and then click Page.

(3) If necessary, click the Left-Hand Page drop-down arrow, and then select the layout of the page you want.

(4) If necessary, click the Right-Hand Page drop-down arrow, and then select the layout of the page you want.

(5) If you want, click More Options to change the default options.

(6) Make your selections, and then click OK.

(7) Click OK.

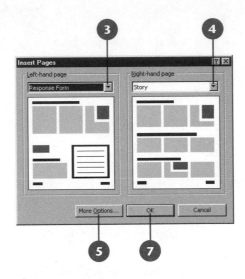

By default, two blank pages are inserted after the current (right-hand) page.

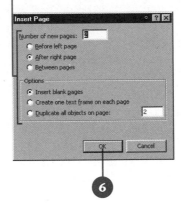

TIP

Delete a page containing a linked text box. *If you delete a page that contains part of a linked text box, the text in the link moves to connected frames on other pages.*

TIP

Insert pages with a mirrored layout. *When you are creating a publication that contains facing pages, such as a book or newsletter, you can use a mirrored-page layout to help keep the publication consistent. Click the Arrange menu, click Layout Guide, and then click the Create Two Background With Mirrored Guides check box.*

SEE ALSO

See "Setting Up Layout Guides" on page 72 for more information on layout guides.

TRY THIS

Delete text in connected frames. *Try deleting a page that contains text continued from another page. Notice what happens to the text when you delete the page.*

Delete a Page from a Two-Page Spread

1. Click the page you want to delete.

2. Click the Edit menu, and then click Delete Page.

3. In Two-Page Spread view, click the option button for the page(s) you want to delete.

   ◆ Click the Both Pages option button to delete both the left and right pages.

   ◆ Click the Left Page Only option button to delete only the left page.

   ◆ Click the Right Page Only option button to delete only the right page.

4. Click OK.

Delete a Page from Single-Page Spread

1. Click the page you want to delete.

2. Click the Edit menu, and then click Delete Page.

3. Click OK.

Changing Paper Size

You can create a wide variety of publications that you can print on many sizes of paper. If you are planning on printing on special sized paper, you can change the paper size setting to match your output. This ability means that your workspace and rulers will accurately reflect your completed product. The default paper size is Letter size because it is the most commonly used. Other available paper sizes are Legal, Commercial-10 Envelope, Executive, and Monarch Envelope.

TIP

Letter size paper. *The most commonly used paper size is 8.5 x 11 inches.*

TIP

See available paper sizes. *See a list of other paper sizes by clicking the Size drop-down arrow in the Print Setup dialog box.*

Change Paper Size

1. Click the File menu, and then click Print Setup.

2. Click the Size drop-down arrow, and then select the paper size you want to use.

3. Click OK.

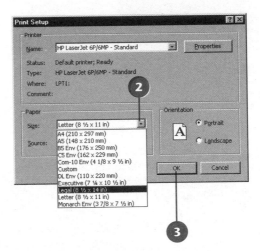

Change the Page Layout

1. Click the File menu, and then click Page Setup.

2. Click the option button for the type of publication layout you're using.

3. Choose the options you want.

4. Click OK.

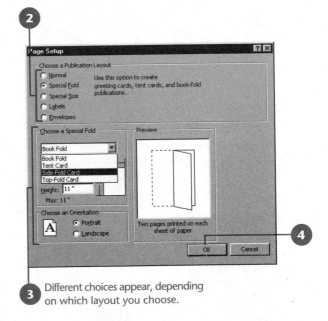

3. Different choices appear, depending on which layout you choose.

Changing Paper Orientation

One factor that affects any publication is the orientation of the printed page. The most commonly used paper orientation is *portrait* (seen in most business letters). In portrait orientation, the length exceeds the width. That same piece of paper can be designed using a *landscape* orientation, in which the width exceeds the length. For example, you would probably use a landscape orientation for a tri-fold brochure.

Change the Paper Orientation

1 Click the File menu, and then click Print Setup.

2 Click the option button you want to use.

- ◆ Click Portrait to print on paper whose length exceeds its width.

- ◆ Click Landscape to print on paper whose width exceeds its length.

3 Click OK.

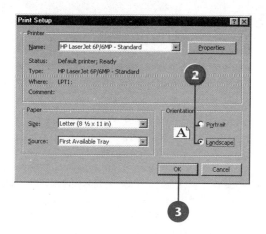

Change the Page Setup

1 Click the File menu, and then click Page Setup.

2 Click the Choose An Orientation option button you want to use.

- ◆ Click Portrait to print on paper whose length exceeds its width.

- ◆ Click Landscape to print on paper whose width exceeds its length.

3 Click OK.

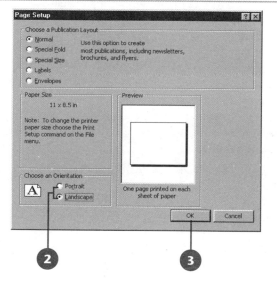

5

Setting Up Layout Guides

Each page of a publication—like any business letter—should have uniform margins. This gives your publication a consistent, professional look. Since a publication is composed of many elements (which may have their own margins), each page is controlled using *layout guides*. Since they are automatically included in each page of a publication, layout guides are located on background pages. In publications with mirrored pages, any adjustment made to one page is automatically reflected on its companion page.

SEE ALSO

See "Adjusting Margins in a Text Frame" on page 78 to see how to change individual frame margins.

Set Up Layout Guides

1. Click the Arrange menu, and then click Layout Guides.

2. Select the value for each of the margin guides you want to adjust.

   ◆ The Left margin guide is the white space at the left of a non-mirrored page.

   ◆ The Right margin guide is the white space at the right of a non-mirrored page.

   ◆ The Top margin guide is the white space at the top of the page.

   ◆ The Bottom margin guide is the white space at the bottom of the page.

3. Click OK.

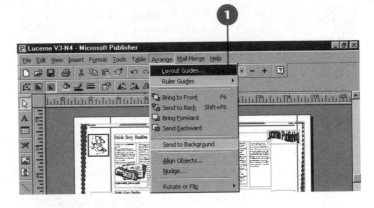

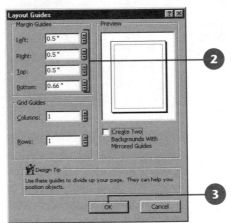

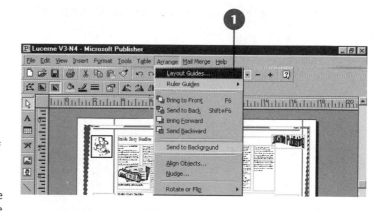

Toggle between background and foreground view. *Switch between background and foreground view by pressing Ctrl+M.*

Set up Grid Guides. *Click the Arrange menu, click Layout Guides, enter the values you want for the grid guides in the Columns and Rows boxes, and then click OK.*

Modify layout guides manually. *Click the View menu, click Go To Background, position the pointer over a layout guide, press and hold Shift, and then drag a layout guide to a new location.*

Create Mirrored Pages

1. Click the Arrange menu, and then click Layout Guides.

2. Click the Create Two Backgrounds With Mirrored Guides check box.

3. Select the value for each of the margin guides you want to adjust.

   ◆ The Inside margin guide is the white space at the inner edge of a mirrored page.

   ◆ The Outside margin guide is the white space at the outer edge of a mirrored page.

   ◆ The Top margin guide is the white space at the top of the page.

   ◆ The Bottom margin guide is the white space at the bottom of the page.

4. Click OK.

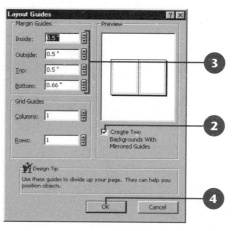

5

Changing the Unit of Measurement

You can use the Measurements toolbar to quickly change the position, size, scaling, rotation, tracking, kerning, and line spacing of objects in Publisher. The up and down arrows on the Measurements toolbar allow you to make exact adjustments which can be difficult sometimes with the mouse pointer.

The unit of measurement determines the ruler display and layout guides used throughout your publication. You can change the default setting—inches—to another available unit of measurement—centimeters, points, or picas—if necessary. (Printers, for example, measure in points.) Choosing another unit of measurement may allow you more flexibility and give you the ability to make finer adjustments.

Change an Object Using the Measurements Toolbar

1. Select the object in which you want to change.

2. Click the View menu, point to toolbars, and then click Measurements to display the toolbar.

3. Click the up or down arrows on the Measurements toolbar you want to change the object.

4. Click the View menu, point to toolbars, and then click Measurements to hide the toolbar.

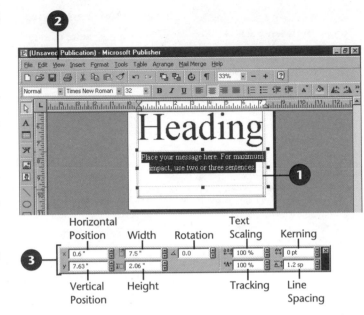

Change Measurement Units

1. Click the Tools menu, and then click Options.

2. Click the General tab.

3. Click the Measurement Units drop-down arrow, and then click a unit of measurement.

4. Click OK.

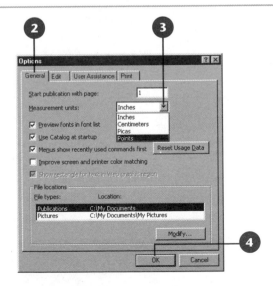

Working with Facing Pages

As your publication grows, you may find it helpful to view facing pages. Viewing facing pages allows you to make more effective and consistent layout changes throughout your publication.

Publisher lets you view your publication using a two- page or single-page spread. You can move between the two views, so use whichever view is best for you.

TIP

Page navigation icons change with page view.
Page navigation icons show the current view. In a two-page spread, mirrored pages appear as left-hand pages and right-hand pages.

Change to Two-Page Spread

1 Click the View menu.

2 Click Two-Page Spread.

A check mark appears next to the option to indicate it is turned on.

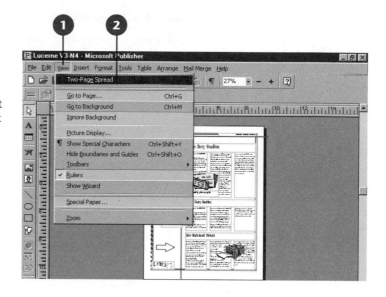

Change to Single-Page Spread

1 Click the View menu.

2 Click Two-Page Spread to deselect it.

The check mark is removed next to the option to indicate it is turned off.

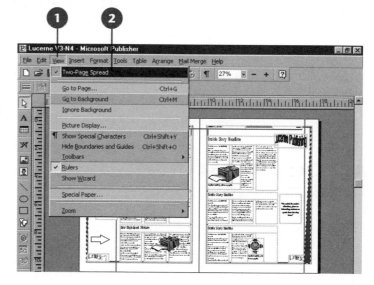

5

Inserting Page Numbers

As a reader, you want to see page numbers on any multi-page publication. Page numbers help you navigate the pages and find specific stories.

You can add a text frame on each page that has a page number, but inserting or deleting pages would mean corrections to the text frame. Use the Page Numbers command in a text frame on background page(s). In the foreground, page numbers will be numbered correctly. When you insert or delete pages, the page numbers are automatically updated.

TRY THIS

Correctly numbered pages.
Once you've added page numbers, add or delete pages and verify that the pages are correctly numbered.

Insert a Page Number

1. Click the View menu, and then click Go To Background.

2. Click the Text Frame Tool button on the Objects bar.

3. Drag the pointer to create a frame.

4. If you want, type any text you want to be included with the page number in the text frame.

5. Click the Insert menu, and then click Page Numbers.

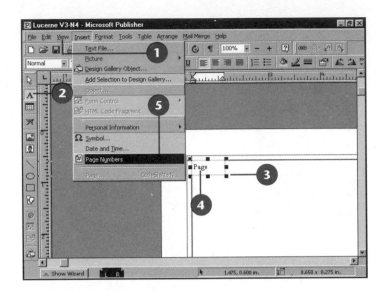

In the foreground, the current page number is displayed.

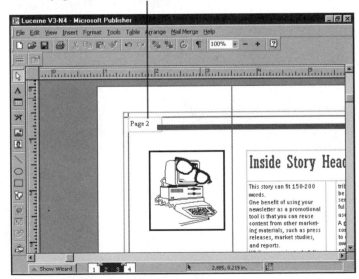

SEE ALSO

See "Background vs. Foreground" on page 107 for information on making changes to the background page(s).

SEE ALSO

See "Changing Font Effects" on page 47 for instructions on applying formatting attributes to text.

Change the Starting Page Number

1. Click the Tools menu, and then click Options.

2. Click the General tab.

3. Click the Start Publication With Page box, and then type the number you want as the first page.

4. Click OK.

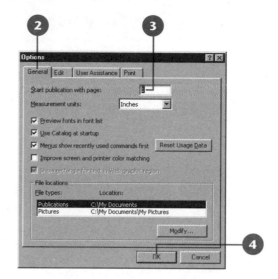

Change the Page Number Format

1. If necessary, switch to the Background view.

2. Select any text you want to change—including the inserted page number symbol.

3. Click buttons on the Formatting toolbar to change the appearance of the text.

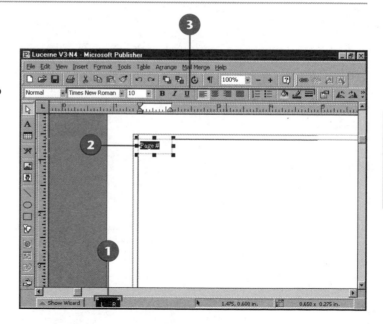

Adjusting Margins in a Text Frame

As you work on individual stories, you may find that you need to make adjustments to margins or to add columns.

Each text frame has a horizontal ruler that displays indent markers that you can use to adjust margins. The indent markers allow you to adjust a paragraph's left indent, right indent, as well as its first and subsequent lines of text.

You can also create columns (and adjust the space between them) in a frame using the Text Frame Properties dialog box.

SEE ALSO

See "Setting Up Layout Guides" on page 72 for instructions on using layout guides.

SEE ALSO

See "Displaying Rulers" on page 52 to learn how to turn a ruler on and off.

Change Text Margins

1. Click the text frame whose margins you want to change.

2. Click and drag the indent markers you want to change.

◆ The First Line Indent marker determines the location of the first character in the first line of a paragraph.

◆ The Hanging Indent marker determines the location of the first character of each remaining line in a paragraph.

◆ The Left Indent marker determines the location of the left margin.

◆ The Right Indent marker determines the location of the right margin.

Left Indent marker   First Line Indent marker   Right Indent marker

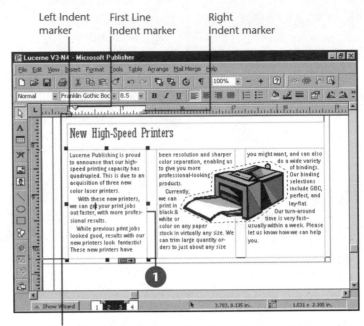

Drag the rectangle to move the Left and First Line indent markers.

Create Columns in a Text Frame

1 Click the text frame in which you want to create columns.

2 Click the Text Frame Properties button on the Formatting toolbar.

3 Click the Columns Number up or down arrows to indicate the number of columns you want, or type the number of columns you want in the text box.

4 Click OK.

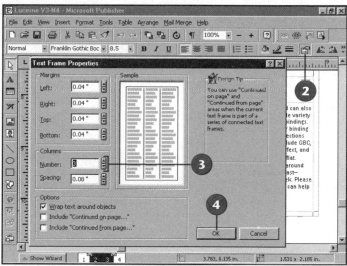

Text Frame Properties button

Adjust the Space Between Columns

1 Click the text frame in which you want to adjust the space between the columns.

2 Click the Text Frame Properties button on the Formatting toolbar.

3 Click the Columns Spacing up or down arrows to change the spacing value, or type the spacing dimension you want in the text box.

4 Click OK.

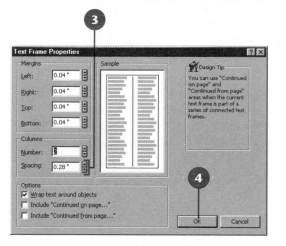

5

Setting Up "Continued" Notices

You can't always count on displaying a story from start to finish, in fact, it may be part of your layout to continue stories on other pages. For this reason, you can use "Continued" notices to help your readers find related story text on other pages.

Publisher automatically updates "Continued" notices when a text frame is moved, or if pages are inserted or deleted.

TIP

Delete "Continued" notices. *Click the text frame, click the Text Frame Properties button, and then clear the Include "Continued" notice(s) check boxes, and then click OK.*

SEE ALSO

See "Inserting Page Numbers" on page 76 for instructions on inserting page numbers.

Set Up "Continued" Notices

① Click the text frame in which you want to add the continued notices.

② Click the Text Frame Properties button on the Formatting toolbar.

③ Click one of the following options:

◆ The "Continued On Page" notice adds a reference line at the bottom of the selected text frame.

◆ The "Continued From Page" notice adds a reference line at the top of the selected text frame.

④ Click OK.

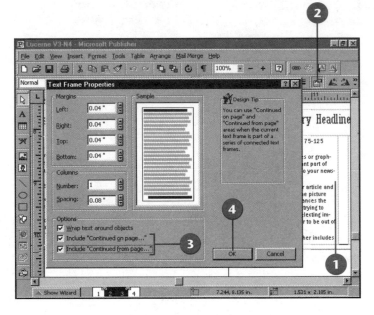

Change a "Continued" Notice Format

① Select the "Continued" notice text you want to change.

② Click buttons on the Formatting toolbar to change the appearance of the text.

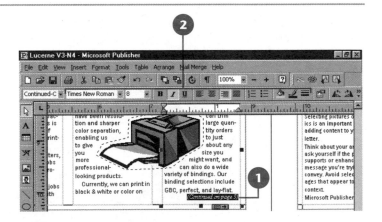

Copyfitting Text

Despite your best efforts, a story may be too long for a text frame. In this case, you can experiment with different font sizes, or you can take advantage of Publisher's AutoFit feature.

AutoFit forces text too long for a specific text frame to fit, a process called *copyfitting*. Once you've selected an AutoFit option, the feature continues to work until you turn it off. This means that you can add or delete text in the frame, and it will always be a perfect fit.

TIP

Edit text. *AutoFit is an impressive feature, but you don't want the text in a frame to be too small to read. Sometimes you just have to edit the text.*

TRY THIS

Copyfit text. *Insert text in a frame you know will be too small. Use the AutoFit feature to make the text fit.*

CopyFit Text

1. Click the text frame whose text you want to fit within the frame.

2. Click the Format menu, and then point to AutoFit Text.

3. Click an AutoFit option.

   ◆ Click Best Fit to shrink or expand text to fit the text frame whenever you resize the frame.

   ◆ Click Shrink Text On Overflow to reduce the point size in the overflow area until there is no text in overflow.

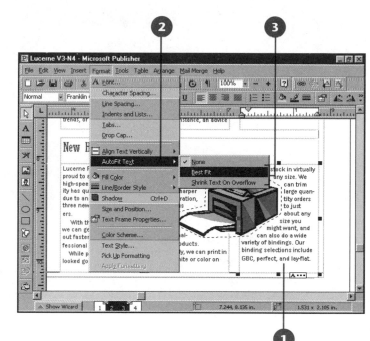

Aligning Text Vertically

You can align text to the top, center, or bottom of its frame. The ability to change the alignment of text can be very helpful when planning and designing captions in a newsletter.

Changing the alignment of text in a frame can add to the visual appeal of captions or headlines, and can add value to your publication.

TRY THIS

Change text alignment.
Change the alignment of text in a frame, and then change the dimension of the frame. See how the text alignment is maintained.

SEE ALSO

See "Copyfitting Text" on page 81 for information on fitting text in a frame.

Align Text Vertically

1. Click the text frame whose text you want to align.

2. Click the Format menu, point to Align Text Vertically, and then click an alignment option.

   ◆ The Top option aligns the text along the upper edge of the text frame.

   ◆ The Center option aligns the text between the upper and lower edges of the text frame.

   ◆ The Bottom option aligns the text along the lower edge of the text frame.

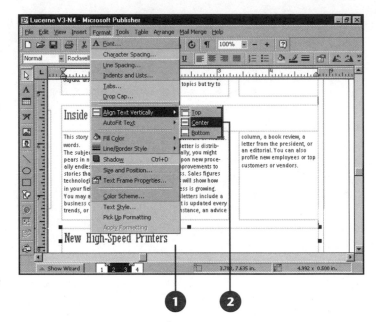

Creating a Table of Contents

If your publication has multiple pages, you'll probably want to make it easy for readers to find specific stories. A table of contents makes this possible.

You can create a table of contents manually or by using the Design Gallery. Create a manual table of contents by drawing a text frame and creating tabs with dot leaders. The Design Gallery contains a wide selection of table of contents styles you can easily add to your publication. Once you've inserted a table of contents in your publication, you can add your own descriptive text and correct page numbers.

SEE ALSO

See "Modifying Your Design Gallery" on page 171 for information on using the Design Gallery.

Use the Design Gallery to Create a Table of Contents

1. Click the page where you want to insert the table of contents.

2. Click the Design Gallery Object button on the Objects toolbar.

3. Click the Table Of Contents category.

4. Click a Table of Contents style.

5. Click Insert Object.

6. If necessary, move the table of contents to its proper location.

7. If necessary, click the Wizard button to make any format changes.

8. Select text in the table and make any necessary changes.

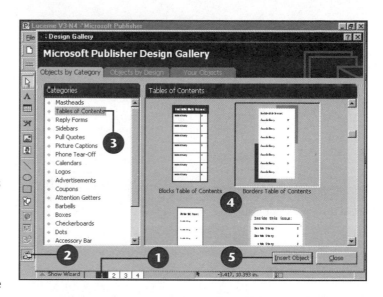

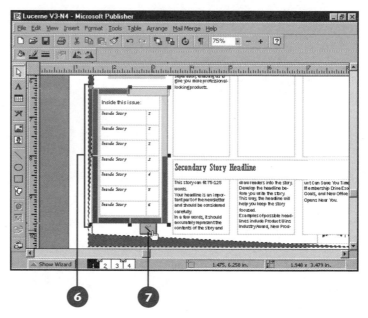

TIP

Dot leaders. *Use dots, called dot leaders, in the Tabs dialog box to connect the left and right sides of your text lines in a table of contents.*

TRY THIS

Create a table of contents. *Use the Design Gallery to create a table of contents for your publication, and then create one manually. Which method do you prefer?*

SEE ALSO

See "Aligning Text with Tabs" on page 53 for information on creating tabs.

Create a Table of Contents Manually

1 Click the Text Frame Tool button on the Objects toolbar.

2 Drag the pointer to create a frame where you want the table of contents to be located.

3 Type a heading (such as "Table of Contents").

4 Continue typing lines of text, pressing Tab to insert the page number.

5 Click the Format menu, and then click Tabs.

6 If necessary, change the tab leaders.

7 Click OK.

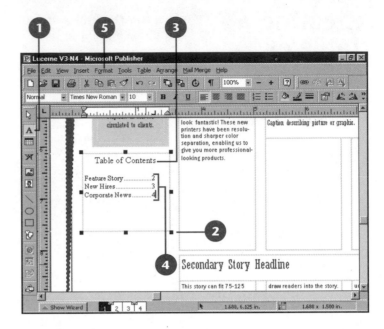

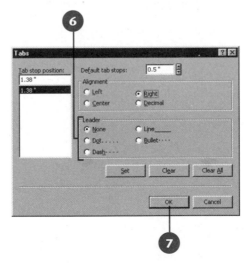

6

Working with Graphics

S pice up any publication by using colorful graphic images that are included with Microsoft Publisher 2000, purchased by you or your company, or created by you using separate graphics software. You can use graphic images to illustrate subject matter or to reinforce a corporate identity in a publication. Used effectively, graphics add value by making your publication look more polished and professional.

Graphics Add Zest to a Publication

In any publication, graphic images force a reader to focus on content. The right number of images—just enough to catch your attention—guides you through a publication from topic to topic. You can add several different types of graphics, such as pictures, shapes, and borders to your publication. You can use the Clip Gallery to insert existing graphics or create your own creative shapes. In addition to creating line borders on images and text boxes, Publisher provides many colorful, artistic borders you can use to surround text and images. In addition, you can use BorderArt to turn any electronic image into an attractive frame border.

Inserting a Picture

Add pictures to a publication to enhance its visual appeal. For example, your company might have a logo that it uses in all its print material. You can also use *clip art*, copyright-free graphics, in your publication to draw attention to a specific topic. In Publisher, a *picture* is any graphic object that you insert as a single unit. You can insert pictures that you've created in a drawing program or scanned in and saved as a file. You can also insert clip art provided with Microsoft Office, that you acquire separately, or that you download from the Clip Gallery Live on the Web. After you insert a graphic object, you can easily delete it if it does not serve your purposes.

TIP

Picture synonyms. *A picture may also be referred to as an object, image, or artwork.*

Insert Clip Art from the Clip Gallery

1. Click the Insert menu, point to Picture, and then click Clip Art.

2. Click the Pictures tab.

3. Click a category in the list.

   Available pictures for the category you selected appear in the list.

4. Click a picture in the category. If necessary, click the down scroll arrow to see all the pictures available in the category.

5. Click the Insert Clip button.

   The picture is inserted in your publication.

6. Click the Close button.

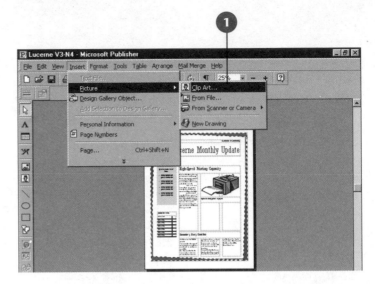

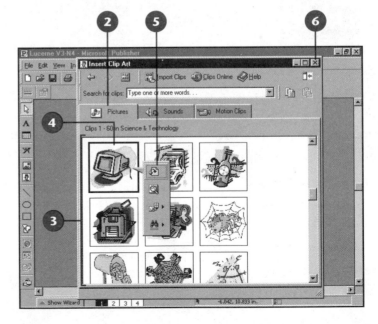

Insert a Picture from an Existing File

1 Click the Insert menu, point to Picture, and then click From File.

2 Click the Look In drop-down arrow, and then select the drive and folder containing the picture you want to insert.

3 Click the graphic image you want.

4 Click Insert.

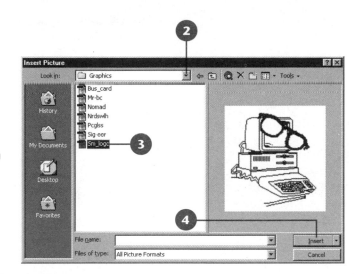

Insert a Picture from Clip Gallery Live

1 Click the Insert menu, point to Picture, and then click Clip Art.

2 Click the Clips Online button. If necessary, establish an Internet connection.

3 Click hyperlinks on the Clip Gallery Live Web site to select the clips you want to insert.

4 When you are finished, click the File menu, click Close, and disconnect from the Internet.

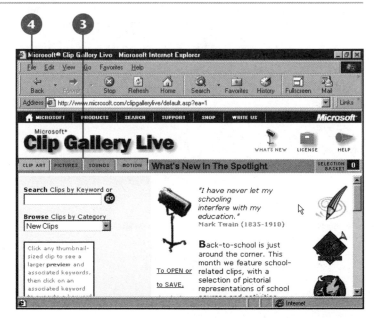

6

Inserting an External Image

You can insert images from a Twain-compatible scanner or digital camera. The ability to generate your own scanned or photographed images means you can use unique images in your publications. Before you can insert an image, you need to install any necessary hardware and software to connect the scanner or digital camera to your computer.

TIP

Resolution and file size.
Experiment with different scanner resolutions. Higher resolution generally leads to crisper images with larger file sizes. Larger image sizes lead to larger publication sizes.

TRY THIS

Generate your own images. *If you have a scanner, scan in a family photo or take one with a digital camera and then insert it into an annual family newsletter.*

Insert an Image from a Scanner or Camera

1 Place the image on the scanning device or take the image using your digital camera.

2 Create or select a picture frame.

3 If necessary, click the Insert menu, point to Picture, point to From Scanner Or Camera, click Select Device, click the device you want to use, and then click OK.

4 Click the Insert menu, point to Picture, point to From Scanner Or Camera, and then click Acquire Image.

5 Start the scanning process using your scanning program.

6 Close the scanning program when you are finished.

The image is added to your publication.

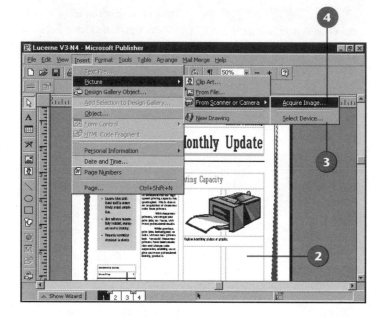

Cropping a Graphic Image

You can crop clip art to isolate just one portion of the picture. Perhaps you have a great photo of several people, including the subject of an article. By cropping the image, you can exclude the additional people in the photo. Clip art from the Clip Gallery is designed so that you can crop, or cut out, even the smallest part of the image and then enlarge it, and the clip art will still be recognizable. You can also crop bitmapped pictures, but if you enlarge the area you cropped, you lose picture detail. You can crop an image by hand using the Crop Picture button on the Formatting toolbar.

Crop an Image Quickly

1️⃣ Click the picture you want to crop.

2️⃣ Click the Crop Picture button on the Formatting toolbar.

3️⃣ Drag the sizing handles until the borders surround the area you want to crop.

4️⃣ Click outside the image when you are finished.

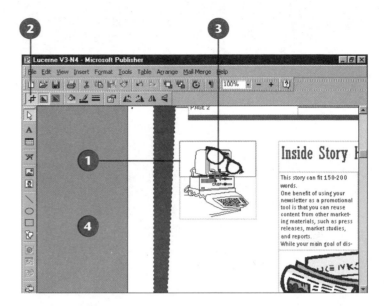

Restore a Cropped Image

1️⃣ Click the picture you want to restore.

2️⃣ Click the Crop Picture button on the Formatting toolbar.

3️⃣ Drag the sizing handles to reveal the areas that were originally cropped.

4️⃣ Click outside the image when you are finished.

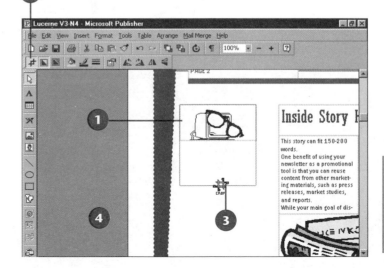

6

Wrapping Text Around an Image

Wrapping text around an image is an effect often seen in newsletters and brochures. This is an effective way of drawing attention to the image, the text, or both. The white space surrounding an image can be adjusted using *wrap points*—the sizing handles (or adjustment handles) surrounding the image—by dragging them toward the center or away from the image. Wrap points let you create a cushion of white space around an image. You can add or delete wrap points using the mouse pointer and Ctrl key.

TIP

Don't overdo it. *There's a fine line between enough text wrap and too much. Too much text wrapping can be distracting and annoying. This feature should be used to add value, not impress your readers.*

Wrap Text Around an Object

1. Click the image you want to wrap text around.

2. Click the Wrap Text To Picture button on the Formatting toolbar.

3. If Publisher asks if you want it to create a new wrap boundary, click Yes.

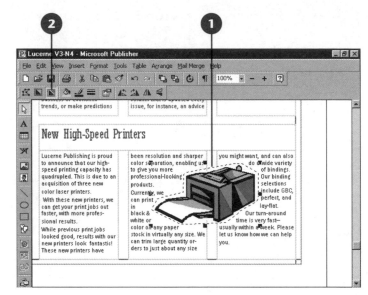

Adjust Wrap Points

1. Click the image whose wrap points you want to adjust.

2. Click the Edit Irregular Wrap button on the Formatting toolbar.

3. Drag any of the handles to new locations.

4. Click the Edit Irregular Wrap button to turn off the feature.

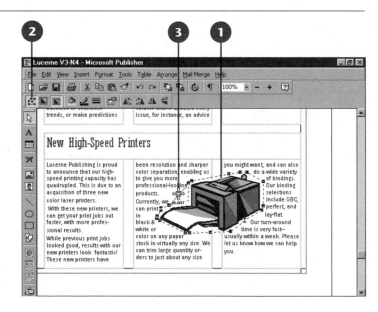

Wrap text around an image. *Insert an irregularly shaped image in text. Then, using the Edit Irregular Wrap feature, adjust the wrap points so the text wraps around the image.*

Preserve white space. *Remember that one principle of good design is to keep white space around an image and throughout a publication.*

Add a Wrap Point

1. Click the image containing wrap points you want to add.

2. Click the Edit Irregular Wrap button to turn on the feature.

3. Press and hold Ctrl, move the pointer over the area where you want to add a new Wrap Point, and then click the Add pointer.

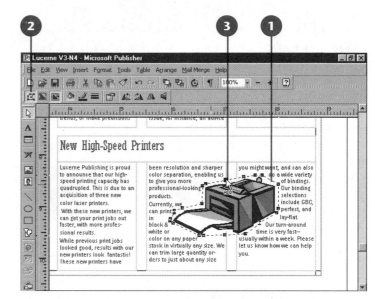

Delete a Wrap Point

1. Click the image containing the wrap points you want to delete.

2. Click the Edit Irregular Wrap button to turn on the feature.

3. Press and hold Ctrl over an existing Wrap Point and then click the Delete pointer.

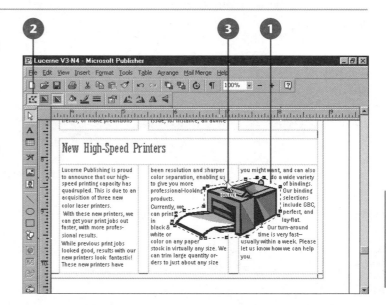

6

Graphics in Publisher's Wizards

Graphics are essential elements within a publication: they provide relief from text and powerfully communicate information.

When you create a publication using a wizard, the publication contains graphic images. While they may not be the images you'll ultimately use in your publication, they serve an important purpose as *placeholders*—temporary images that help you design your layout and determine where stories and images should be placed. Publisher also lets you create your own *smart objects*. These are logos, coupons, ads, or calendars that are created by an additional wizard. Smart objects have a Wizard button within the object that appears when the object is clicked. You can create smart objects during the catalog selection process, or separately using the Design Gallery.

Smart objects can also be *synchronized*. This means that when you make changes are made to them, Publisher also makes the changes in similar objects so you don't have to change each object individually.

Placeholder image created by Publisher.

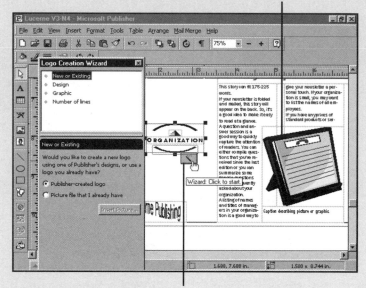

Click the Wizard button to create the smart object.

Recoloring an Image

Although your own artwork, and that provided by Publisher, is very attractive, you may want to change the coloring. You might want to alter colors so an image fits in with an existing color scheme or complies with publication issues.

When you recolor an image, all the colors are changed to a single color or shades of a single color. You can, however, preserve any occurrences of black within the image while still changing a color.

TIP

Retain black within an image. *Black elements within an image add a much-needed contrast to an image.*

Recolor an Image

1. Click the image you want to recolor.

2. Right-click the image, and then point to Change Picture on the shortcut menu.

3. Click Recolor Picture.

4. Click the Color drop-down arrow, and then click a color you want. If necessary, click More Colors to see additional color choices.

5. Click an option button to either recolor the whole picture or to leave black parts black.

6. Click OK.

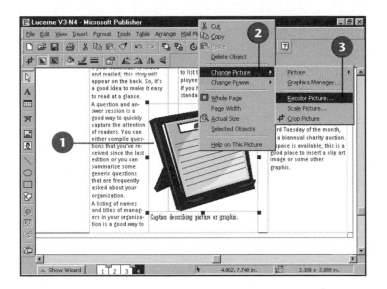

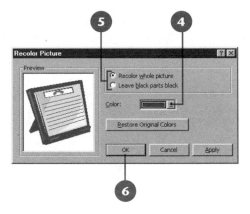

Drawing a Line or Border

Lines or borders can make any document more attractive. In a publication, they serve as visual guides that help a reader focus on specific elements. To call attention to a specific story, you could surround it with a border. A well-placed vertical line provides a visual definition of a column and can be incorporated into a publication's style. The default line or border color is black, but you can change it to any color you choose.

Draw a Straight Line

1 Click the Line Tool button on the Objects toolbar.

2 Drag the pointer to draw the line until the object is the shape and size that you want.

To make the line straight, press and hold Shift while you drag.

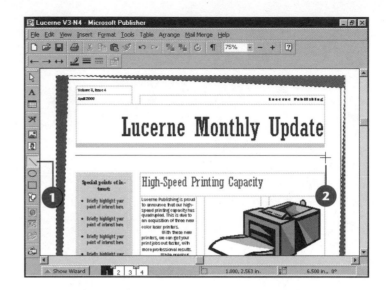

Change Line Style

1 Click the line you want to edit.

2 Click the Line/Border Style button on the Formatting toolbar.

3 Click the style you want, or click More Styles to see additional choices.

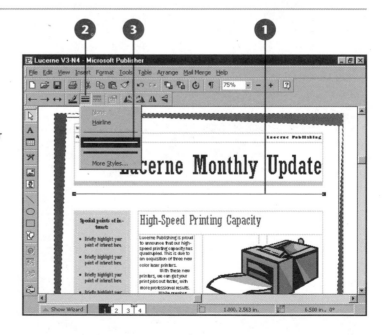

Create a Border

1. Right-click the image to which you want to add the border, and then point to Change Frame on the shortcut menu.

2. Point to Line/Border Style.

3. Click the style you want, or click More Styles to see additional choices.

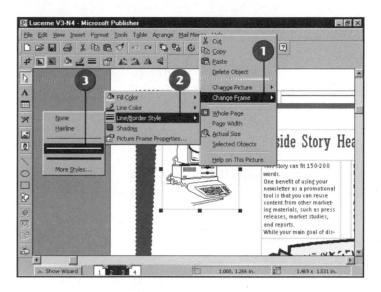

TRY THIS

Create a colorful border.
Create a border around a frame. Then experiment with different colors and line widths to see what looks best.

Change a Line or Border Color

1. Click the line or border whose color you want to change.

2. Click the Line Color button.

3. Click the color you want, or click More Colors to see additional choices.

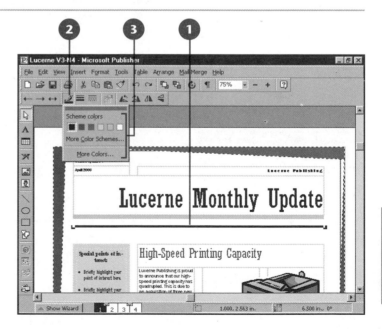

Working with BorderArt

In addition to line borders, you can also use artwork to create customized borders using BorderArt. *BorderArt* is a feature that uses graphic images to create a border effect. BorderArt comes with a large number of borders all ready for use in your publication. You can also turn any graphic image into BorderArt. For example, you might have a logo you want to use as a border.

TRY THIS

Change the size of BorderArt. *Select a BorderArt image and then click the Border Size up and down arrows to adjust the size. Notice how the border's appearance changes.*

Apply BorderArt

1. Right-click the frame to which you want to apply BorderArt.

2. Point to Change Frame (or Change *shape name* if you're applying BorderArt to an object other than a frame).

3. Point to Line/Border Style, and then click More Styles.

4. Click the BorderArt tab.

5. Click one of the Available Borders.

6. If you want, click the Border Size up and down arrows to make the border larger or smaller.

7. If you want, click the Color drop-down arrow to change the border color.

8. Click OK.

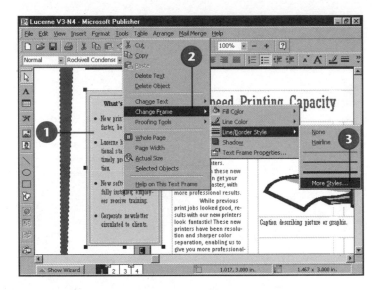

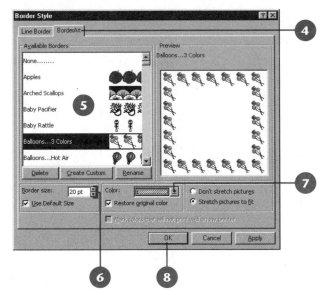

Create Custom BorderArt

1. Right-click the frame to which you want to add BorderArt.

2. Point to Change Frame (or Change *shape name* if you're applying BorderArt to an object other than a frame).

3. Point to Line/Border Style, and then click More Styles.

4. Click the BorderArt tab.

5. Click Create Custom.

6. Click Choose Picture.

   The Insert BorderArt dialog box is displayed.

7. Click a category in the list, click an image, and then click Insert Clip.

   The Name Custom dialog box is displayed.

8. Type a name for your border, and then click OK.

9. Click OK.

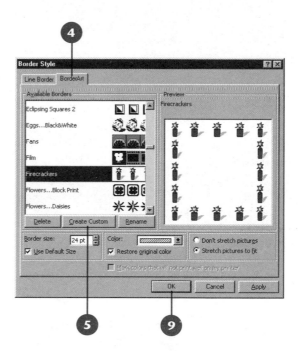

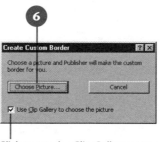

Click to use the Clip Gallery as an art source.

Drawing Custom Shapes

You can choose from many different Custom Shapes, ranging from bursts to lightening bolts, to draw on your publications. The two most common Custom Shapes, the oval and rectangle, are available directly on the Objects toolbar. You can view and select the rest of the Custom Shapes by clicking the Custom Shapes button on the Objects toolbar. Once you have drawn a Custom Shape, you can resize it using the sizing handles.

TIP

Draw a circle or square. *To draw a perfect circle or square, click the Oval Tool button or Rectangle Tool button on the Objects toolbar, and then press and hold the Shift key as you drag to draw the shape.*

Draw an Oval or Rectangle

1. Click the Oval Tool button or Rectangle Tool button on the Objects toolbar.

2. Drag the pointer to draw the oval or rectangle until the object is the shape and size that you want.

   The shape you draw takes on the default line and fill color.

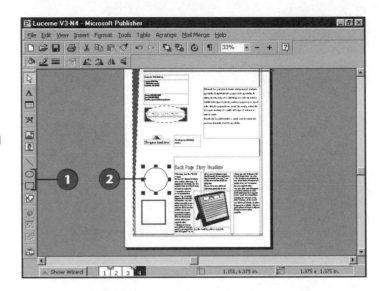

Draw a Custom Shape

1. Click the Custom Shapes button on the Objects toolbar.

2. Click the shape you want.

3. Drag the pointer to draw the oval or rectangle until the object is the shape and size that you want.

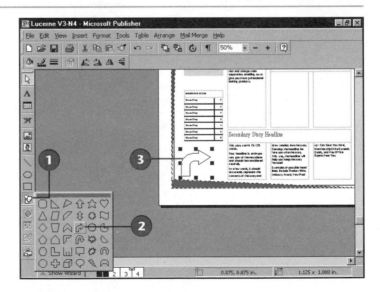

TRY THIS

Change the size of a Custom Shape. *Once you've created a custom shape, resize it while maintaining its scale by pressing and holding Shift as you drag one of its handles.*

SEE ALSO

See "Rotating and Flipping an Object" on page 114 for information on rotating and flipping an object.

Resize a Custom Shape

1. Click the custom shape you want to resize.

2. Click one of the sizing handles, and then drag the handle to change the size of the custom shape.

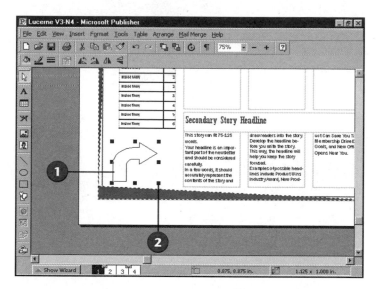

Add a Shadow to a Custom Shape

1. Click the custom shape to which you want to add a shadow.

2. Right-click the shape, and then point to Change Shape on the shortcut menu.

3. Click Shadow.

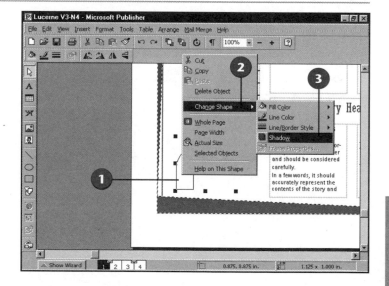

6

Changing Object Colors

When you create a drawing object, it takes on the default color and fill effect. You can change the fill color and effect using colors, tints or shades, patterns, and gradients. You can use these features to create your own logos. Depending on the project you are working on, you might want to use colors and patterns to create a specific effect that attracts the reader's attention.

SEE ALSO

See "Drawing a Line or Border" on page 94 for instructions on changing line color.

Change the Fill Color

1. Click the object whose fill color you want to change.

2. Click the Fill Color button on the Formatting toolbar.

3. Click the fill color you want, or click More Colors to see additional color choices.

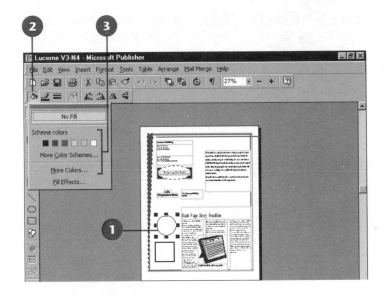

Change the Fill Effect

1. Click the object whose fill effect you want to change.

2. Click Fill Color button on the Formatting toolbar.

3. Click Fill Effects.

4. Click the Style option button you want.

5. Click the style fill effect you want.

6. Click the drop-down arrow, and then select the base color or secondary color you want.

7. Click OK.

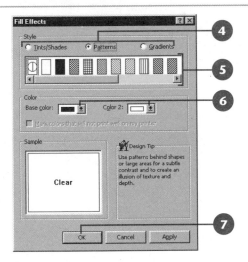

Changing the Shape of an Object

Once you draw an object, you might need to change its shape. You can resize an object using the mouse by dragging a sizing handle to a new location. You can gain more precise control over an object's size and position using the Format menu to specify the exact location and size of the drawn object.

TIP

Nudge an object. *Once selected, you can* nudge *an object—move it slightly—by pressing any of the arrow keys while pressing and holding Alt.*

Use a Sizing Handle to Change a Shape

1. Click the object to be resized.

2. Drag one of the sizing handles.

   ◆ To resize the object in either the vertical or horizontal direction, drag a sizing handle on the side of the object.

   ◆ To resize the object in both the vertical and horizontal directions simultaneously, drag a sizing handle on the corner of the object.

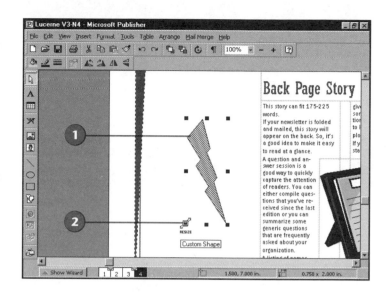

Resize an Object Precisely

1. Click the object to be resized.

2. Click the Format menu, and then click Size And Position.

3. Click the Size Width and Height up or down arrows to resize the object.

4. Click OK.

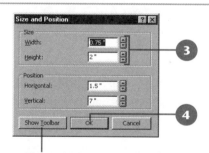

Click to display a toolbar with more precise measurement capabilities.

6

Drawing an Arrow

Perhaps your publication has a coupon or important notice you want to call attention to. An arrow is the perfect device to use to draw a reader's attention to a particular item. You can create an arrow using the Line Tool or Custom Shapes button. When you use the Line Tool, you can decide on which end—or both ends if you prefer—the arrowhead should appear. When you use the Custom Shapes button to draw an arrow, you can create a larger object that you can fill with color or patterns.

Draw an Arrow Shape

1. Click the Custom Shapes button on the Objects toolbar.

2. Click the arrow shape.

3. Drag the pointer to draw the arrow until it is the shape and size that you want.

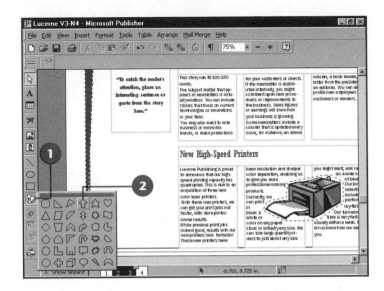

Add an Arrowhead to a Line

1. Click the Line Tool button on the Objects toolbar.

2. Drag the pointer to draw the line until the object is the shape and size that you want.

3. Click the arrowhead on the Formatting toolbar you want to apply to the line.

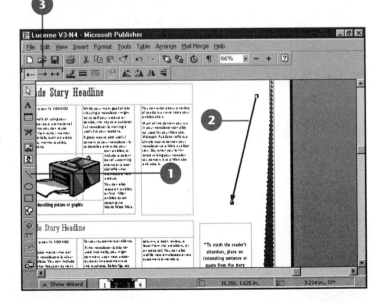

SEE ALSO

See "Changing Object Colors" on page 100 for information adding colors and fill patterns to an object.

Custom Rotate button

Change the Shape of an Arrow

1. Click the arrow shape you want to change.

2. Drag one of the sizing handles.

   ◆ To resize the object in either the vertical or horizontal direction, drag a sizing handle on the side of the object.

   ◆ To resize the object in both the vertical and horizontal directions simultaneously, drag a sizing handle on the corner of the object.

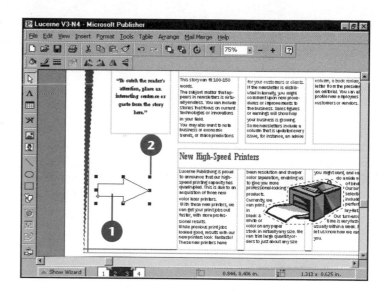

Change Arrow Direction

1. Click the arrow shape you want to changed.

2. Click the Custom Rotate button on the Standard toolbar.

3. Click the Left or Right Rotation buttons.

4. Click Close.

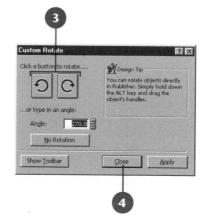

6

Managing Graphic Images

Most publications have so many graphic images, it can be hard to keep track of them all. Using Publisher's Graphics Manager, an outside printing service can have complete information about all the graphic images found within a publication. The *Graphics Manager* provides information about each image's name, type, status (whether it is linked or embedded), and location within the publication. In addition, the status of each image can be modified from within the Graphics Manager. This ability makes it easier for outside printers to control image sources.

TIP

Image manipulation.
Sometimes when a printing problems occur, an outside printing source might need to create a link to an embedded object or to export an enhanced object in your publication.

Track Graphic Images

1. Click the Tools menu, and then point to Commercial Printing Tools.

2. Click Graphics Manager.

3. Click an image in the list.

4. Click a button to create or break a link, update a graphic image, or get details on an image.

5. Click Close.

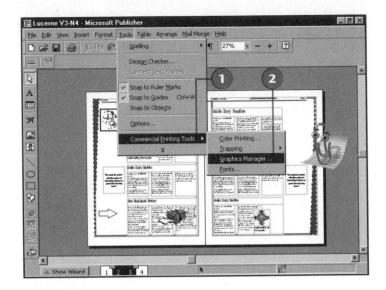

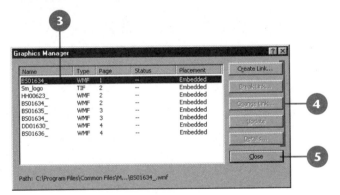

7

Enhancing Your Design

Your publication will look professionally designed when you enhance it with graphic images and apply Microsoft Publisher 2000 color schemes. Color—which plays a more important role than ever before—is a crucial part of any publication. Publisher provides a wide variety of predesigned color schemes from which you can choose. These color schemes are professionally coordinated and can be chosen when the publication is initially created or at any time during the design process.

Using Design Enhancing Tools

Many multipage publications repeat information such as page numbers, mastheads, or logos. Instead of requiring you to arrange these elements on each page, Publisher's publications contain foreground and background pages. You can use background pages to insert repetitive information without making entries on each page. You can layer objects within a publication so certain shapes appear to be in front of, or behind, other objects. Once you've perfected the appearance of multiple objects, you can *group* them so they behave as if they are a single object. You can *ungroup* multiple objects at any time so they return to their original individual components. In addition, you can align objects with other objects, or rotate or flip them to suit your needs.

Choosing a Color Scheme

Color is an important element in any publication. For some businesses, color is used to establish an identity or image. Color can also be used to set a mood within a publication, suggesting that it is serious or light-hearted. Publisher includes more than 60 sets of carefully coordinated color schemes. If this is not enough, you can create and save your own color scheme. Apply a color scheme to a publication at any time, not just when you create it.

TRY THIS

Apply a color scheme to an existing publication. *Open an existing publication and try applying other color schemes to it.*

Apply a Standard Color Scheme

1. Click the Format menu, and then click Color Scheme.

2. Click the Standard tab.

3. Scroll through the available schemes, and then click the scheme you want.

4. Click OK.

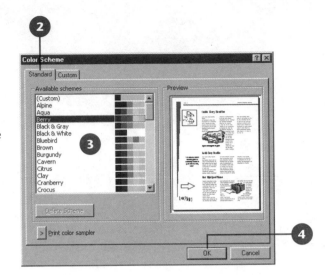

Apply a Custom Color Scheme

1. Click the Format menu, and then click Color Scheme.

2. Click the Custom tab.

3. Click the New drop-down arrow for the main or accent colors, and then select the new colors you want.

4. Click Save Scheme.

5. Type a name in the Type A Name For Your Custom Color Scheme box, and then click OK.

6. Click OK.

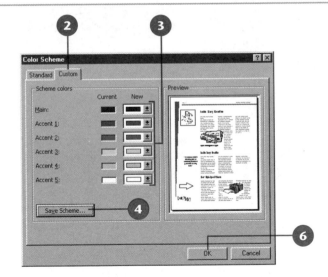

Background vs. Foreground

Each page in a publication has a foreground and a background. Publications with odd and even pages have odd and even background pages. Publisher makes it easy to work with repetitive information that you place on each page. If you want page numbers or a logo to appear on each page, put them on a background page. If you choose to use a watermark, you can also place it on a background page. Whether your publication has four or forty pages, storing information on background pages means more efficient, consistent-looking pages.

Information on a background page can be edited only when the background pages are visible. You can toggle back and forth between background and foreground pages using the View menu, or by pressing Ctrl+M. Background images can be ignored on any given page by clicking the View menu and then clicking the Ignore Background command.

This image placed on the background appears on each left page.

A message appears when you click a background image while you're in foreground view.

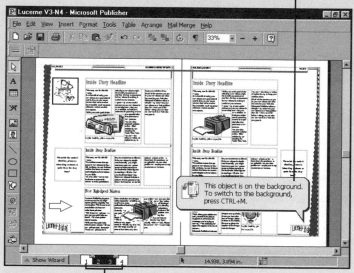

Indicates these are background pages.

This background image appears on each right page.

Page number icons indicate these are foreground pages.

Grouping Objects Together

As you work with multiple objects—particularly those you create yourself—you may want to combine several objects into one. Suppose you created a logo using a variety of drawn shapes. Once you've arranged the objects, you can combine them—or *group* them—so they are easier to copy or move. Grouped objects have one set of sizing handles and can be grouped or ungrouped again as necessary.

TIP

Group objects with the right mouse button. *Once objects are selected, you can group them by right-clicking, and then clicking Group Objects on the shortcut menu.*

Group Objects

1. Click an object to select it.

2. Press and hold the Shift key as you click each object you want to group together.

3. Click the Group Objects button.

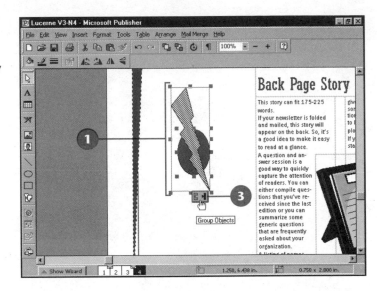

Ungroup Objects

1. Click the grouped object you want to ungroup.

2. Click the Ungroup Objects button.

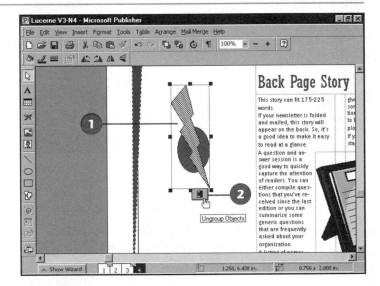

Layering Objects

When working with multiple objects, you might need to consider how they are layered. Layers let you create the illusion of dimension: that one object is in front of, or behind, another. If objects overlap, the most recently created drawing will be placed on top of older drawings, but you can change how the objects are ordered, or layered. You can move an object to the extreme front or back of other objects, or you can move one object at a time to create a unique layering effect.

TIP

Group layered objects.
Once you've layered objects the way you want them, group them so their order will be maintained.

Move an Object to the Front or Back

1. Click the object whose layer position you want to change.

2. Click the layer button you want to use.

   ◆ Click Bring To Front to layer the selected object on top of all other objects.

   ◆ Click Send To Back to layer the selected object beneath all other objects.

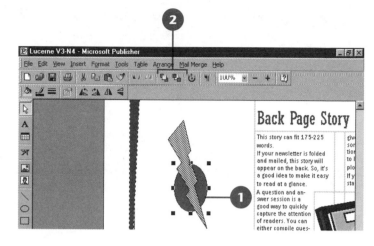

Move an Object One Layer

1. Click the object whose layer position you want to change.

2. Click the Arrange menu, and then click the layer option you want to use.

   ◆ Click Bring Forward to send the selected object one layer in front of its current location.

   ◆ Click Send Backward to send the selected object one layer behind its current location.

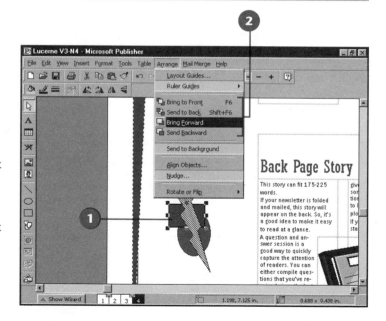

Aligning Objects

Often when you work with multiple objects, they look their best when aligned relative to one another, or to a margin or ruler guide. For example, you can align three objects so their tops match along an invisible line. Objects can be aligned left to right, top to bottom, or any combination of these.

Align Objects Left to Right

1. Press and hold the Shift key while clicking each object you want to align.

2. Right-click the selected objects, and then click Align Objects on the shortcut menu.

3. Click a Left To Right option button.

4. Click OK.

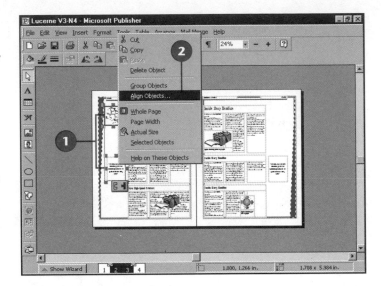

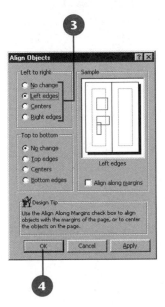

Align Objects Top to Bottom

1. Press and hold the Shift key while clicking each object you want to align.

2. Right-click the selected objects, and then click Align Objects on the shortcut menu.

3. Click a Top To Bottom option button.

4. Click OK.

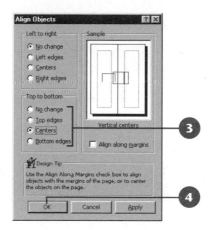

SEE ALSO

See "Aligning with Precision" on page 112 for information on using Snap To Guides.

Align Along Margins

1. Press and hold the Shift key while clicking each object you want to align.

2. Right-click the selected objects, and then click Align Objects on the shortcut menu.

3. Click to select the Align Along Margins check box.

4. Click a Top To Bottom or Left To Right option button or both.

5. Click OK.

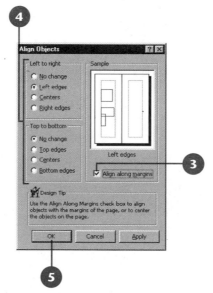

Aligning with Precision

Not only can you align objects with each other, you can create controls within a publication that help you align objects. You can create an unlimited number of *ruler guides*, green vertical and horizontal lines you place on a page, to help you line up any objects you choose.

Ruler guides can be moved and deleted as you see fit, can be placed on foreground and background pages, and can vary from page to page. Once in place, an object appears to have a magnetic attraction to a ruler guide due to the Snap To feature.

TIP

Move a ruler. *Move a ruler by placing the pointer over a ruler guide, and then pressing and holding Shift while dragging the ruler to a new location.*

Create a Ruler Guide

1 Press and hold the Shift key while dragging the pointer away from a ruler.

◆ Drag from the vertical ruler to create a vertical guide.

◆ Drag from the horizontal ruler to create a horizontal guide.

2 Release the mouse button and Shift key when the guide is in position.

Press Shift and drag the pointer away from a ruler to create a ruler guide.

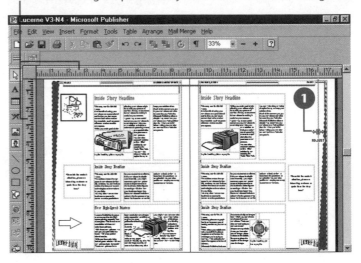

Snap an Object to a Guide

1 If necessary, click the Tools menu, then click Snap To Guides to turn the feature on.

2 Click the object you want to snap to a ruler guide.

3 Drag the object towards the ruler guide.

4 Release the mouse button once the object snaps to the guide.

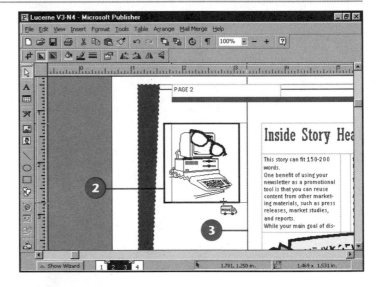

7

Delete a ruler guide. *Press and hold Shift while dragging a ruler guide back to its vertical or horizontal ruler to delete the guide.*

See "Aligning Objects" on page 110 for information on lining up multiple objects.

Nudge an object with the keyboard. *You can also nudge a selected object by pressing and holding Alt while pressing one of the keyboard arrow keys.*

Turn off Snap To Guides

1 Click the Tools menu.

2 Click Snap To Guides to turn the feature off.

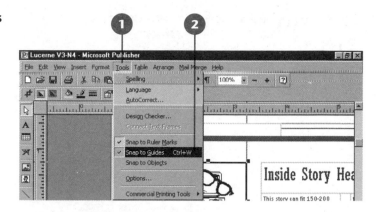

Nudge an Object

1 Click the object you want to nudge.

2 Click the Arrange menu, and then click Nudge.

3 Click the Nudge control arrow buttons until the object is positioned the way you want it.

4 Click Close.

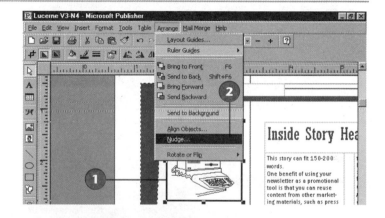

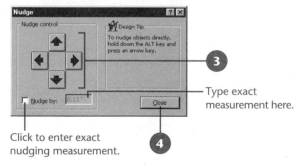

Type exact measurement here.

Click to enter exact nudging measurement.

Rotating and Flipping an Object

You can change the orientation of a drawing object by rotating or flipping it. For example, if you want to create a mirror image of your object, you can flip it. To turn an object on its side, you can rotate it 90 degrees. Rotating and flipping tools work with drawing and text objects.

In most cases, drawn objects can be rotated and flipped; graphic images (such as clip art or graphic images) can only be rotated.

TIP

Rotate an object 90 degrees. *To rotate an object 90 degrees to the left, click the Rotate Left button on the Formatting toolbar. To rotate an object 90 degrees to the right, click the Rotate Right button on the Formatting toolbar.*

Custom Rotate an Object

1. Click the object you want to rotate.

2. Click the Custom Rotate button on the Standard toolbar.

3. Click the left or right rotation buttons to rotate the object in 5 degree intervals.

4. Click Close.

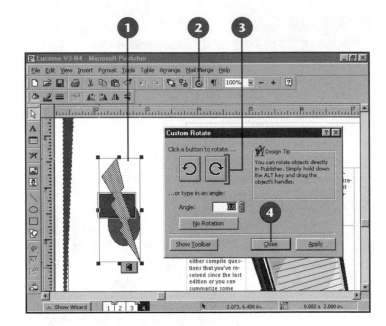

Flip an Object Horizontally

1. Click the object you want to flip horizontally.

2. Click the Flip Horizontal button on the Formatting toolbar.

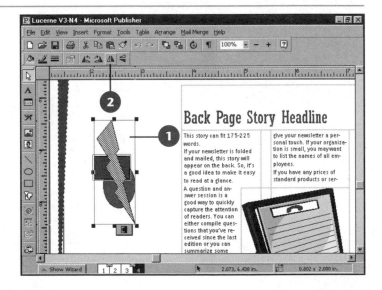

Flip an Object Vertically

1. Click the object you want to flip vertically.

2. Click the Flip Vertical button on the Formatting toolbar.

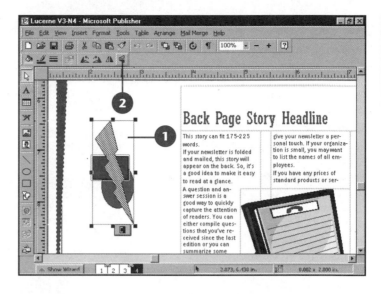

Rotate an Object

1. Click the object you want to rotate.

2. Click the Rotate Left or Rotate Right button on the Formatting toolbar to rotate the object 90 degrees.

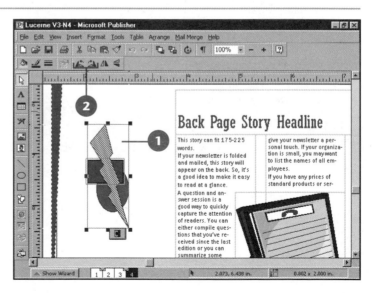

Evaluating Your Design

You can create error-free publications using the Design Checker. This feature identifies common problems such as too many colors or fonts, or images that may be too large for Web viewing. Once the Design Checker identifies problems, it suggests solutions, which you can accept or ignore. You determine Design Checker's settings in its Options dialog box.

TIP

Check spelling. *The Design Checker does not check spelling. For a perfect publication, you also need to run the spelling checker.*

TIP

Learn from mistakes. *Take notes on problem areas found by the Design Checker and use them to avoid mistakes in your next publication.*

Check a Design

1. Click the Tools menu, and then click Design Checker.

2. Click an option button for the pages you want to check.

3. If you want, click Options to change Design Checker parameters.

4. Click any options buttons or check boxes in the Options dialog box, and then click OK.

5. Click OK.

6. Click the Ignore, Ignore All, Continue, Close, or Explain buttons as the Design Checker evaluates your publication.

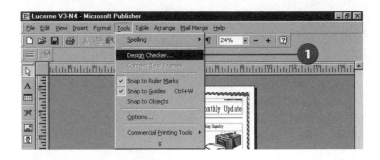

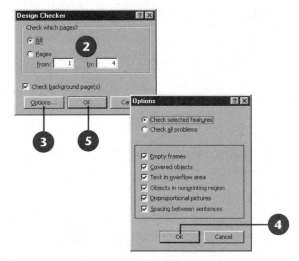

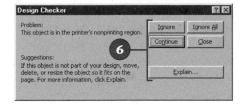

Ensuring Consistency with Synchronization

Consistency is one element that separates an average publication from one that is truly professional. For example, a logo that appears in many places in a newsletter should have the same appearance throughout the publication. A poster with telephone number tear-offs should have the same phone number on all tags.

Publisher makes it easy to create such elements and keep them consistent—even if you modify them later on. Using a technique called *synchronization*, elements created with a wizard or in the Design Gallery will always be identical. Synchronized elements are linked to one another within their current publication. If you change one synchronized element, all its companion objects are changed simultaneously.

Provided the elements are created using a wizard or the Design Gallery, Publisher can synchronize personal information components, logos, calendars, phone tear-offs, newsletter running headers and footers, Web navigation bars, and graphic accents.

A SUMMARY OF SYNCHRONIZED ELEMENTS		
If you created	Using	Synchronizes
Logo	Design Gallery	The content of text and picture frames, and all formatting attributes in all copies on pages.
Personal information component	Wizard, or Personal information	Changes appearance of text on all pages of the current document.
Multipage yearly calendar	A Wizard	Changes appearance of the month names, days of the week, and dates

Working with Synchronization

When you change the formatting of certain objects, such as smart objects, or change personal information components, Publisher makes the change to other similar objects in the publication. This is called *synchronization*. You can turn synchronization on or off for synchronized objects within a publication. When you change a synchronized object, *all* the linked elements, including color schemes, are changed. Since consistency in a publication is so important, elements 'in-sync' always reflects the content changes that you make.

Turn On Synchronization

① Click the Tools menu, and then click Options.

② Click the User Assistance tab.

③ Click the Click To Reset Wizard Synchronizing button.

④ Click OK.

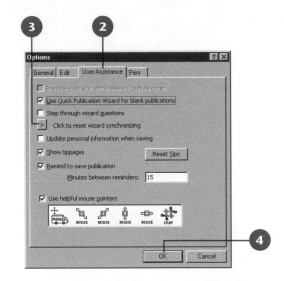

Edit a Synchronized Element

① Click the synchronized element you want to edit.

② Make your change(s).

- ◆ Enter new text in a text frame.
- ◆ Insert a new image in a picture frame.
- ◆ Change formatting attributes.

③ Click anywhere outside the element to deselect it.

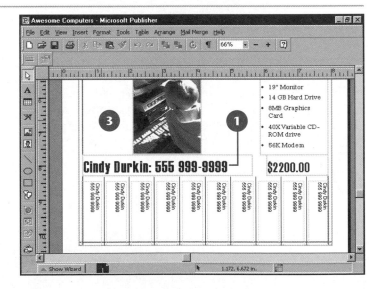

Creating WordArt

WordArt is a feature available in Microsoft Publisher 2000—and shared by many other Microsoft programs—that you can use to create highly stylized text. Use the objects created in WordArt as logos or decorations throughout any publication.

Making Creative Text Objects

With WordArt, you can create beautiful objects that would only have been available to clients of professional design firms several years ago. Even though the results contain text, they are objects with all the characteristics of clip art or any other graphic image in your publication. Using easy-to-understand toolbar buttons, you can create objects containing text (such as a company or product name) that assumes interesting shapes and sizes. You can change the shape at any time, as well as apply formatting attributes, colors, and patterns. Like other objects, you can wrap story text around a WordArt object, and enhance the object itself using special effects, alignment, and spacing techniques. You can also rotate WordArt shapes and modify the actual shape using a slider control.

Creating WordArt

WordArt is a Microsoft program you can use to stylize text in your publication. Unlike text in a story, each WordArt you create is an object—like any other graphic image. WordArt provides a wide variety of text styles that can have dynamic patterns and effects. All you have to do is type the text and apply some stylistic effects. For example, if you don't have a logo for your company, you can easily create one using WordArt.

TIP

Use the Insert menu to insert WordArt. *You can also insert WordArt using a menu. Click the Insert menu, click Object, click the Create New option button, click Microsoft WordArt 3.2, and then click OK.*

Create WordArt

1 Click the WordArt Frame Tool on the Objects toolbar.

2 Position the pointer where you want the object in the publication. Drag to draw a rectangle with the pointer where you want the object.

3 Type the text you want in the Enter Your Text Here dialog box.

4 If you want, click the Shape drop-down arrow to change the WordArt shape.

5 Use any of the WordArt toolbar buttons to create interesting effects.

6 To deselect the WordArt, click anywhere on the publication, or press Esc.

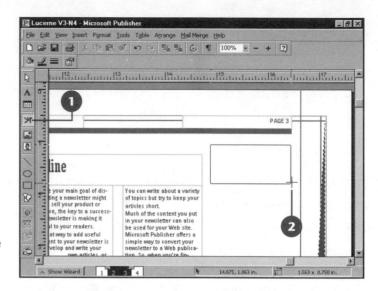

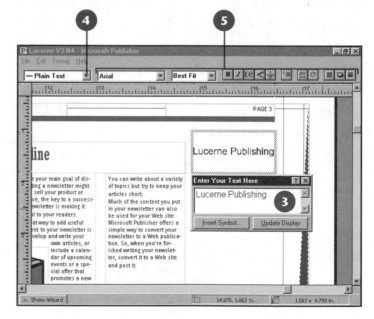

Using the WordArt Toolbar

WordArt adds a special dimension to text. Unlike plain text, WordArt's dazzling appearance makes words seem to jump off the page. Using waves and curves, WordArt assumes shapes not usually seen in standard text.

Everything you need to make beautiful WordArt creations is contained on the WordArt toolbar. Many of the possible effects will seem familiar: colors, patterns, fonts, font sizes, and text attributes (such as bold and italics). Many effects may also be new: making upper and lower-case characters the same height, changing text orientation, modifying character spacing, and stretching text to fit a frame.

The toolbar buttons are the same regardless of how you open WordArt. For an existing object, you can open WordArt by double-clicking or right-clicking the object, pointing to Change Object, pointing to Microsoft WordArt 3.2, and then clicking Open.

8

USING WORDART TOOLBAR BUTTONS		
Button	**Name**	**Description**
— Plain Text ▼	Shape drop-down arrow	Changes WordArt shape
Arial ▼	Font drop-down arrow	Changes typeface of text
Best Fit ▼	Fit drop-down arrow	Changes text size
B	Bold	Changes text to bold
I	Italic	Changes text to italics
Ee	Upper/Lower-Case	Makes uppercase and lowercase letters the same height
◁	Orientation	Changes direction of text
A	Stretch	Changes how text fits in the frame
≡	Center Align	Changes alignment of object
AV	Character Spacing	Modifies spacing between characters
C	Rotate	Rotates an existing object
◪	Color/Pattern	Changes colors or patterns used in the object
◘	Shadow	Adds shadow effect to the object
≡	Line width	Changes width of a line

Editing WordArt Text

Once you create a WordArt object, you can change it to suit your needs. Like text, WordArt can contain letters, numbers, and symbols. As you're working on your publication, you might want to change wording within a WordArt object or add a symbol. Once you've changed a WordArt object or added symbols, WordArt applies any previous formatting to the modifications.

SEE ALSO

See "Creating WordArt" on page 120 for more information about creating a WordArt object.

TIP

Evaluate text and shapes.
The length of text used within WordArt can be critical. Text that is too long can make WordArt hard to read. Text that is too short may make it hard to see certain shapes.

Add Text to WordArt

1. Double-click the WordArt object to open it.

2. Click the text box to position the insertion point, and then add or edit the text.

3. Click Update Display.

4. Click a blank area of the publication to deselect the WordArt object.

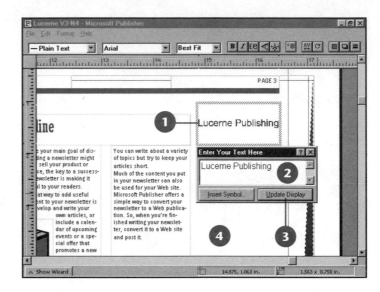

Insert a Symbol in WordArt

1. Double-click the WordArt object to open it.

2. Click the text box to position the insertion point, and then click Insert Symbol.

3. Click a symbol.

4. Click OK.

5. Click Update Display.

6. Click a blank area of the publication to deselect the WordArt object.

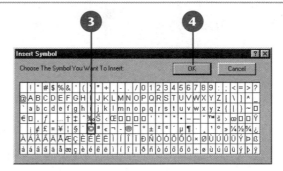

TIP

Make one change at a time. *When making changes to a WordArt object, see how each change affects the appearance of the object. This method makes it easier to "retrace your steps" and return the object to its original appearance.*

TIP

Right-clicking vs. double-clicking. *When you open the WordArt window by right-clicking, all the same elements and options are displayed—although in a different format—as when you double-click a WordArt object.*

Open WordArt by Right-Clicking

1. Right-click the WordArt object.

2. Point to Change Object, point to Microsoft WordArt 3.2, and then click Open on the shortcut menu.

3. Make any changes to the WordArt object.

4. Click OK.

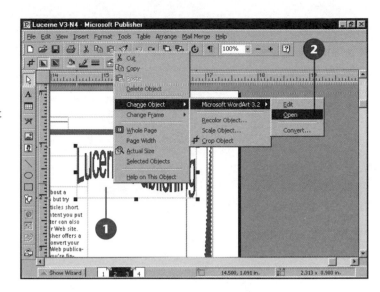

Changing WordArt Font and Size

Like text in a document, you can change the font and font size used within WordArt. A *font* is a collection of letters and numbers with similar styling characteristics. Fonts are grouped in two main groups: serif and sans serif. A *serif* is a small line found at the bottoms or ends of characters. Fonts typically found in publication text use a serif font—such as Times New Roman. Headlines tend to use a *sans serif* (without serifs) font such as Arial.

TIP

Measuring characters. *Each character is measured in points. A point is 1/72 of an inch.*

Change the WordArt Text Font

1. Double-click the WordArt object to open it.

2. Select the text you want to format in a different font.

3. Click the Font drop-down arrow on the WordArt toolbar.

4. Click a font from the list.

5. Click Update Display.

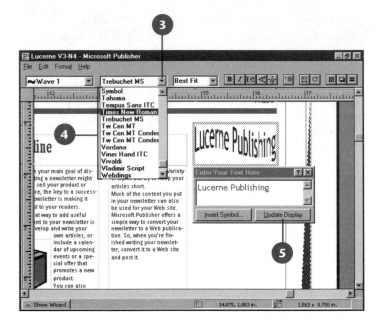

WordArt should add value.
Make sure any WordArt object is legible. WordArt should enhance your publication, not just impress readers with your skills.

Let WordArt size the text.
The Best Fit option lets WordArt determine the best text size for the WordArt.

Change the WordArt Text Size

1. Double-click the WordArt object to open it.

2. Select the text you want to change to a different font size.

3. Click the Fit drop-down arrow on the WordArt toolbar.

4. Click a size from the list.

5. If necessary, click Yes to resize the frame or No to leave the frame the size it is.

6. Click Update Display.

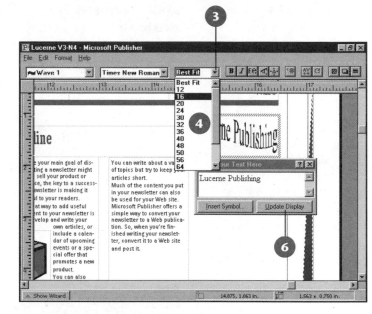

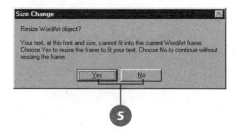

Formatting WordArt Text

You can use formatting attributes, such as bold or italics, to make characters stand out and achieve a more dramatic look. Applying some of the same text formatting found in most word-processing programs can enhance WordArt text. Apply formatting attributes with the click of a toolbar button. You can also change the orientation of WordArt text, stretch WordArt to fit its frame, and apply mixed-case formatting, in which uppercase and lowercase characters are the same height.

SEE ALSO

See "Changing WordArt Font and Size" on page 124 for instructions on changing an object's font and font size.

Apply Formatting Attributes

1. Double-click the WordArt object to open it.

2. Click a formatting attribute button on the WordArt toolbar.

   ◆ Click Bold to give text a darker, thicker appearance.

   ◆ Click Italic to give text a slanted, more delicate appearance.

3. Click Update Display.

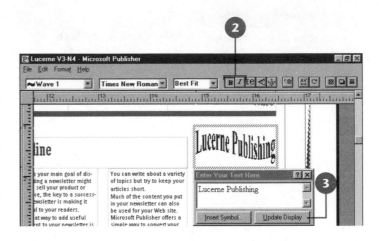

Apply Mixed-Case Formatting

1. Double-click the WordArt object to open it.

2. Click the Upper/Lower Case button on the WordArt toolbar.

3. Click Update Display.

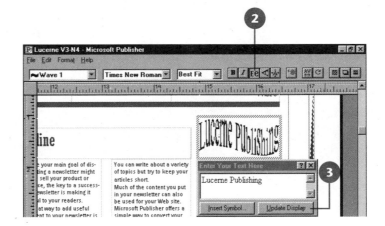

TIP

WordArt toggle buttons.
*Some WordArt toolbar
buttons—such as Orientation
and Stretch—are toggle buttons.
Turn them on and off by
clicking the same button.*

Change WordArt Orientation

1 Double-click the WordArt object to open it.

2 Click the Orientation button on the WordArt toolbar.

3 Click Update Display.

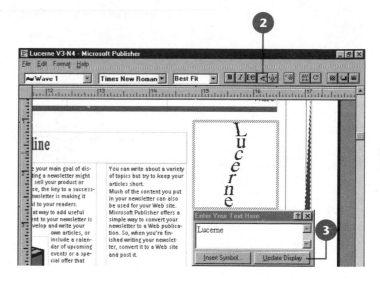

Stretch WordArt to Fit its Frame

1 Double-click the WordArt object to open it.

2 Click the Stretch button on the WordArt toolbar.

3 Click Update Display.

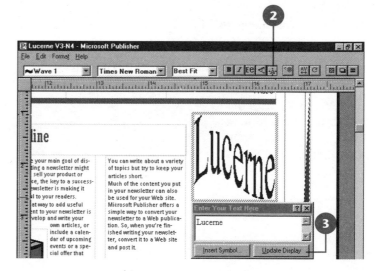

8

Rotating WordArt Text

Modifying the rotation of WordArt can dramatically change the way it looks. You can change the orientation of WordArt by rotating the text within the WordArt object or by rotating the object itself.

If you choose to rotate the WordArt text, you modify the angle of the text. As you change the rotation, you'll see the text tilt change. As you change the slider control, you'll see the WordArt shape change.

Rotating the WordArt object does not alter the contents or shape of the WordArt. It does, however, change the rotation of the entire object.

Rotate Text in WordArt

1. Double-click the WordArt object to open it.

2. Click the Rotate button on the WordArt toolbar.

3. Click the Rotation up or down arrows to change the text angle.

4. Click the Slider up or down arrows to change the shape effect.

5. Click OK.

6. Click Update Display.

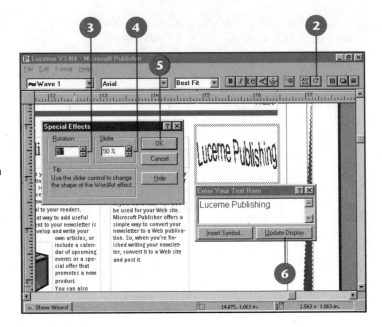

Rotate WordArt

1. Double-click the WordArt object to open it.

2. Click the Custom Rotate button on the Standard toolbar.

3. Click the left or right rotation buttons, and then click the Angle up or down arrows to change the angle of the object.

4. Click Close.

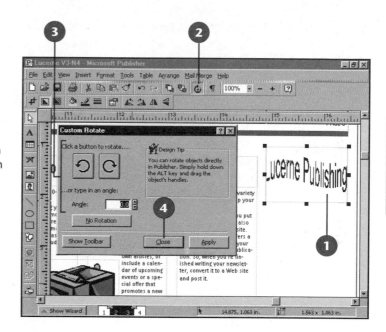

Changing the WordArt Shape

You can change the shape of any WordArt object by using the Shape drop-down arrow. The Shape palette displays 36 different WordArt shapes that you can apply to your object. Changing the shape of any WordArt object can enhance your publication and draw your reader's eye to a particular story. You might want to change the shape of a WordArt object to make a series of words easier to read or to identify a certain shape with your company or business.

Change the Shape of WordArt Text

1. Double-click the WordArt object to open it.

2. Click the Shape drop-down arrow on the WordArt toolbar.

3. Click a shape on the palette.

4. Click Update Display.

5. Click a blank area of the publication to deselect the WordArt object.

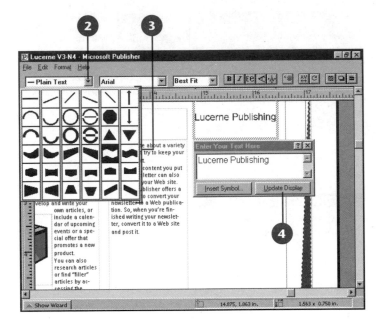

Controlling Alignment

You can align WordArt text to create unique effects. Use alignment control to change the spacing between and within words.

For instance, you can use the Word Justify feature to add spaces between words *without* affecting the character spacing. The Letter Justify feature inserts spaces between each character. The Stretch Justify feature elongates the appearance of characters, without actually adding spaces between them.

Justify WordArt Text

1. Double-click the WordArt object to open it.

2. Click the WordArt Alignment button on the WordArt toolbar.

3. Click a justification option.

   ◆ Click Stretch Justify to stretch the appearance of characters instead of adding spaces between them.

   ◆ Click Letter Justify to insert spaces between characters.

   ◆ Click Word Justify to leave character spacing within words intact by inserting space between words.

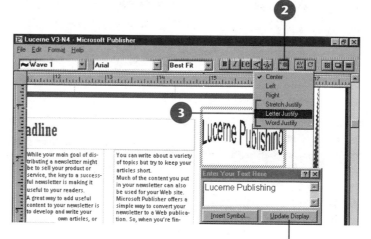

Click here when you want to view the results of your changes.

Align WordArt

1. Double-click the WordArt object to open it.

2. Click the WordArt Alignment button on the WordArt toolbar.

3. Click an alignment option.

4. Click Update Display.

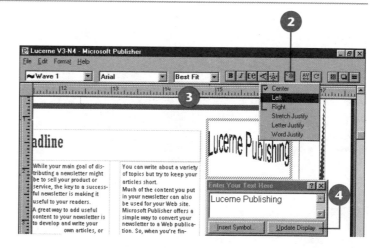

Applying Special Effects

You can apply a number of special effects to your Word-Art object. These effects, such as adding color or fill patterns, adding outlines to letters, and applying a shadow, can give dimension to WordArt and can really make it stand out.

By default, WordArt characters are shown in solid black with a black border. If you have access to a color printer, you can take advantage of all the available colors and patterns. In Publisher, you can also change the object's foreground and background colors.

Adding a shadow to WordArt can make it look unique: the shadow effect is determined by the object's shape.

Add Color to WordArt

1. Double-click the WordArt object to open it.

2. Click the Color/Pattern button on the WordArt toolbar.

3. If you want, click the Foreground drop-down arrow, and then select a color.

4. If you want, click the Background drop-down arrow, and then select a color.

5. Click OK.

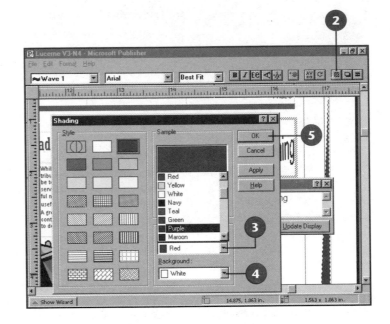

Add a Fill Pattern to WordArt

1. Double-click the WordArt object to open it.

2. Click the Color/Pattern button on the WordArt toolbar.

3. Click a shading style.

4. Click OK.

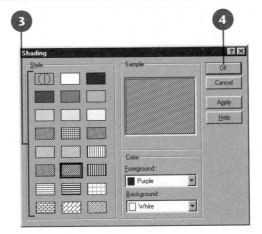

Modify the Outline of Letters

1. Double-click the WordArt object to open it

2. Click the Line Width button on the WordArt toolbar.

3. Click a border thickness.

4. If you want, click the Color drop-down arrow, and then select a color.

5. Click OK.

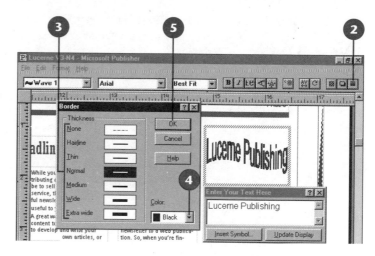

Apply a Shadow to WordArt

1. Double-click the WordArt object to open it.

2. Click the Shadow button on the WordArt toolbar.

3. Click a shadow style.

4. If you want, click the Shadow Color drop-down arrow, and then select a color.

5. Click OK.

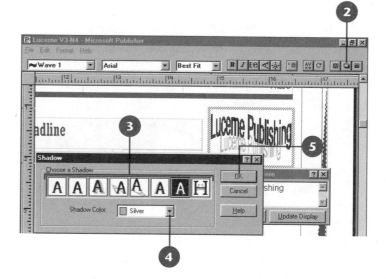

Enhancing WordArt

As you become more familiar and comfortable working with WordArt, you may want to experiment with character spacing and text wrapping.

You may have noticed that the spacing between characters sometimes doesn't look quite right. There may be too much space between certain letters, or perhaps too little. Adjusting the spacing between characters is known as *kerning*. Adjusting the spacing between lines is known as *leading*. You can also change the properties of any object using the Object Frame Properties button.

SEE ALSO

See "Controlling Alignment" on page 131 for information on other alignment and character spacing options.

Adjust Spacing Between Characters

1. Double-click the WordArt object to open it.

2. Click the Format menu, and then click Spacing Between Characters.

3. Click a Tracking option button.

4. Click OK.

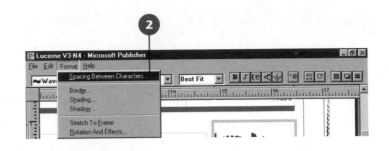

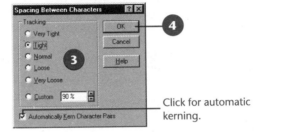

Click for automatic kerning.

Wrap Text Around WordArt

1. Double-click the WordArt object to open it.

2. Click the Wrap Text To Frame or Wrap Text To Picture button on the Formatting toolbar.

3. If necessary, click Yes for Publisher to create a new wrap boundary.

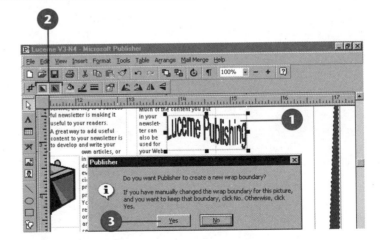

Change Frame Properties

1. Double-click the WordArt object to open it.

2. Click the Object Frame Properties button on the Formatting toolbar.

3. Click a Wrap Text Around option button.

   ◆ Click Entire Frame to have text wrap around the top, bottom, left, and right of your frame. Adjust the distance from each edge using the Margin up or down arrows.

   ◆ Click Picture Only to have the text "hug" the frame. Adjust the distance from the image edge using the Outside up or down arrows.

4. Click OK.

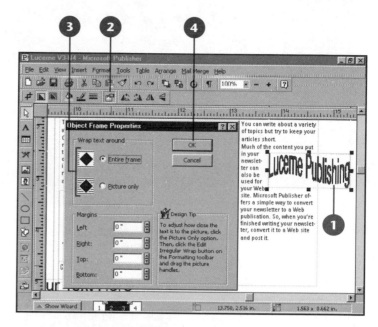

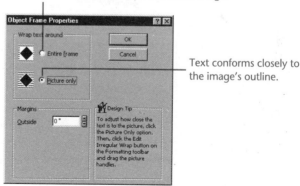

Text forms a rectangular shape around an image.

Text conforms closely to the image's outline.

Resizing a WordArt Object

Once you have the appearance of your WordArt the way you want it, you can resize it just like any other object.

You can resize WordArt using the mouse or by changing the object. To stretch any object while maintaining its original proportions, hold down the Ctrl key while you drag a sizing handle. Resizing with the mouse is based on your visual assessment of the object's appearance, whereas scaling using Publisher's Scale Object dialog box is a more precise method.

TIP

Scale using the Format menu. *You can also open the Scale Object dialog box by clicking the Format menu and then clicking Scale Object.*

Resize WordArt

1. Click the WordArt object to select it.

2. Place the pointer over a sizing handle and drag until the outline is the correct size.

   ◆ Drag a sizing handle to change the frame size without regard to proportions.

   ◆ Press and hold the Ctrl key while dragging to maintain the object's current proportions.

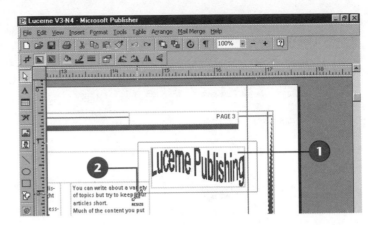

Scale WordArt

1. Right-click the WordArt object, point to Change Object, and then click Scale Object on the shortcut menu.

2. Type the percentage of scale height and width.

3. Click OK.

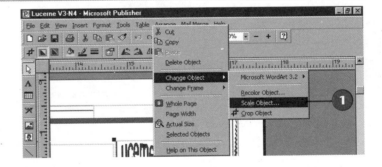

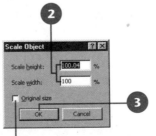

Click to return image to original scaling.

9

Creating Tables

Tables are a great way to organize information in a publication. The column and row structure helps draw attention to important data and make the information easier to read, whether it's a price list, store hours, a resume, team scores, or a table of contents.

Building the Table You Want

Like text, every table included in a publication must be in a frame. You decide how many columns and rows you need when you draw the table frame. As you work, you can modify the table to have more or fewer columns and rows. After you enter text in the table, you then choose just the right format to enhance its content. Try one of Microsoft Publisher 2000's predesigned formats, modify a predesigned format, or create your own from scratch. As a final touch, size the table to fit your publication perfectly. If you've already entered the text or created the table in another Windows-based document, don't reinvent the wheel. Instead, import the table rather than redoing it.

Table Components

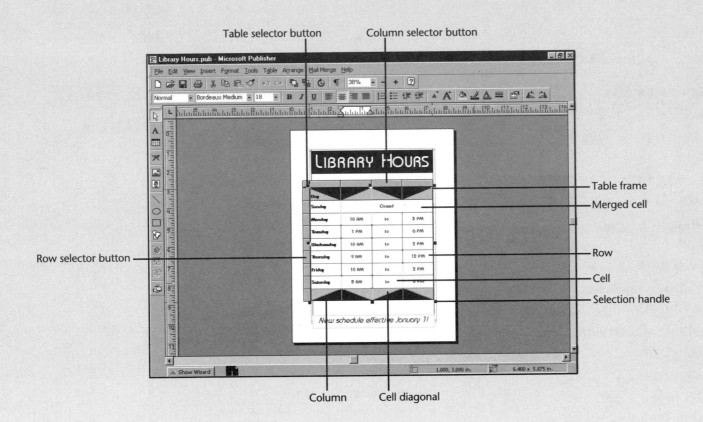

Table selector button

Column selector button

Row selector button

Table frame

Merged cell

Row

Cell

Selection handle

Column

Cell diagonal

Creating a New Table

Many types of information are easier to arrange in tables. Think of such information as price lists, score results, product specifications, store hours, and even calendars and tables of contents. *Tables* are grids of vertical columns and horizontal rows. You create a table by first drawing its *frame*, or structure. Draw the outside borders, then specify the number of rows and columns you want, and finally, choose an appropriate table format.

Create a Table Frame

1 Click the Table Frame button on the Objects toolbar.

2 Position the pointer where you want the upper-left corner of the table to appear.

3 Drag diagonally down to where you want the lower-right corner of the table to appear.

The Create Table dialog appears.

4 Enter the number of rows and columns you want in the table.

5 Select a table format.

6 Click OK.

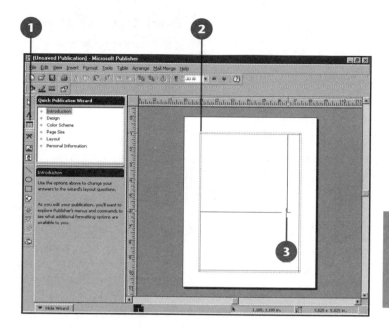

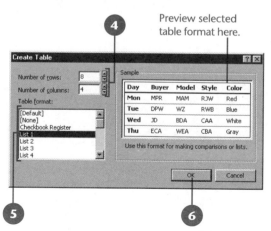

Preview selected table format here.

Entering Text into Table Cells

You enter text into an existing table frame one cell at a time. A *cell* is the box created by the intersection of a column and row. Each cell acts like a mini-text frame. You can quickly copy text from a selected cell to one or more selected cells either to the right or below the original cell.

TIP

Lock a table. *If you don't want the table to expand, you can lock the table. Click in the table, click the Table menu, and then click Grow To Fit Text to remove the check mark, if necessary.*

TIP

Table expands to fit your text. *As you type text in cells, the table grows to accommodate the characters you enter if it is unlocked.*

Enter Text into a Cell

1. Click the cell in which you want to add text.

2. Type the text you want to appear in that cell.

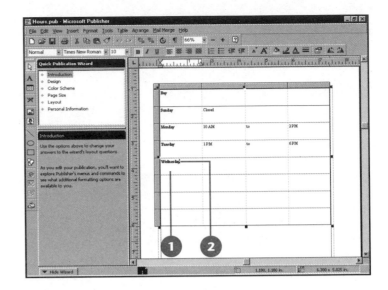

Insert Identical Text into Several Cells

1. Click the cell you want to copy.

2. Drag to select the cell or cells you want to paste the text into either below or to the right of the cell.

3. Click the Table menu, and then click Fill Down to copy the text to cells below, or click Fill Right to copy the text to cells to the right.

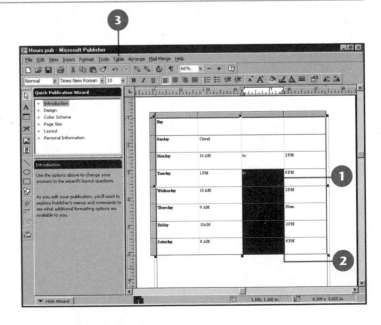

Copy or move text to nonadjacent cells. *Select the cell or cells you want to copy or move, and press Ctrl+C to copy the text or Ctrl+X to cut the text. Select the cell or cells (in the same number or pattern) where you want to copy the text and press Ctrl+V to paste the text.*

Drag and drop text to other cells. *Select the cell whose text you want to copy or move. To copy, press and hold Ctrl as you drag the selected text to a new cell. To move, drag the selected text to new a cell. Release the mouse button and Ctrl, if necessary.*

Zoom the view. *If you can't see the text you enter, press the F9 key to enlarge the view.*

Disappearing text. *If you add more text than fits in a table cell, Publisher puts the extra text in an overflow area where you can't see it. To see it, manually format the text or table until it fits, or unlock the table so it grows to fit.*

Move Around a Table

Enter and edit text in a cell in the same way you would enter and edit text in a text frame. The insertion point shows where text you type will appear in a table. Refer to the table for methods of moving from cell to cell.

MOVING FROM CELL TO CELL	
To Move	Do This
To any cell, or to text within a cell	Click in the cell or text.
To the next cell	Press Tab.
To the preceding cell	Hold down Shift and press Tab.
Forward one character or cell	Press the right arrow key.
Backward one character or cell	Press the left arrow key.
Up one row or cell	Press the up arrow key.
Down one row or cell	Press the down arrow key.

9

Selecting Parts of a Table

Once you create your table frame and column and row structure, you enter text into cells just as you would in a text frame. The first row in the table is good for column headings, whereas the leftmost column is good for row labels. To enter text in cells, you must move around the table. Knowing how to select the rows and columns of a table is also essential to working with the table itself. You must select cells and text in order to format them, enter text, delete unnecessary text, and add or remove rows and columns. A *range* is a group of two or more adjacent cells.

Select Table Parts

Refer to the table for methods of selecting table parts, including:

◆ The entire table

◆ One or more rows and columns

◆ One or more cells

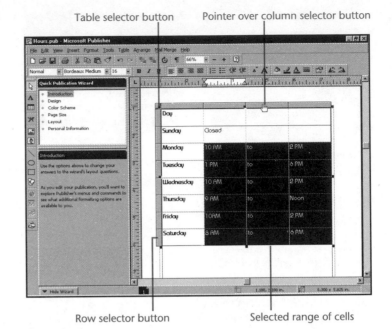

Table selector button   Pointer over column selector button

Row selector button   Selected range of cells

SELECTING TABLE PARTS

To Select	Do This
A single cell	Drag over the cell.
A range of cells	Drag from the cell in the upper-left corner of the range to the cell in the lower-right corner of the range.
One or more rows	Click the row selector button for the first row you want to select, and then drag to select the row selector buttons for the other rows you want.
One or more columns	Click the column selector button for the first column you want to select, and then drag to select the column selector buttons for the other columns you want.
The entire table	Click the table selector button.

Apply text formats. *You can format text in a table cell just as you format text in a text frame. Just select the text you want to format and then apply a new font, size, color, and so on.*

Format cells. *Select one or more cells and change the font, size, position, and alignment just as you would text in text frames.*

See "Changing the Font and Size of Text" on page 46 and "Changing Font Effects" on page 47 for more information about formatting text.

Different pointers. *As you select table parts with the pointer, the pointer shape changes. When you position the pointer over a row or column selector button, the pointer becomes a pointing hand. When you position the pointer within a cell to select text, the pointer becomes an I-beam.*

Select Text in a Table

Refer to the table for methods of selecting text in a table, including:

♦ One word

♦ Part of the text in a cell

♦ All the text in a cell

SELECTING TEXT IN A TABLE	
To Select	Do This
One word	Double-click the word.
Some text in a cell	Drag the I-beam pointer across the text.
All text in a cell	Click in the cell and press Ctrl+A.

Selected text in cell   I-beam pointer

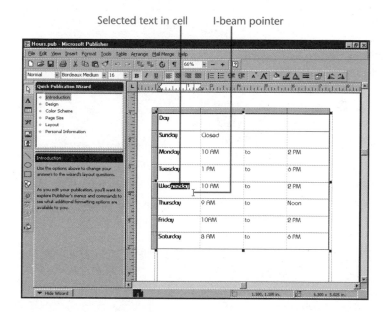

9

Choosing a Table Format

Publisher comes with a variety of table designs (called *formats*) you can choose from. They include formats for presenting numbers or financial data, making comparisons or lists, and preparing tables of contents. Each has a special combination of text formatting and alignments as well as cell and table patterns, shading, and borders. You can modify these formats if necessary. You can quickly copy all the formatting from one cell to other cells with the Format Painter.

Choose a Table Format

1. Click in the table you want to format.

2. Click the Table menu, and then click Table AutoFormat.

3. Click a format.

4. Click Options.

5. Click the various formatting option check boxes to select or deselect them.

6. Click OK.

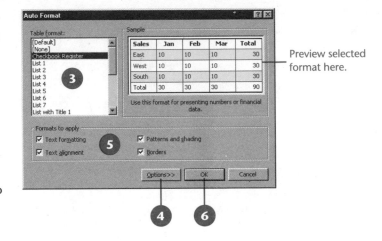

Preview selected format here.

Copy a Cell's Format

1. Select the cell whose format you want to copy.

2. Click the Format Painter button on the Standard toolbar.

3. Click the cell or drag across a range of cells whose format you want to change.

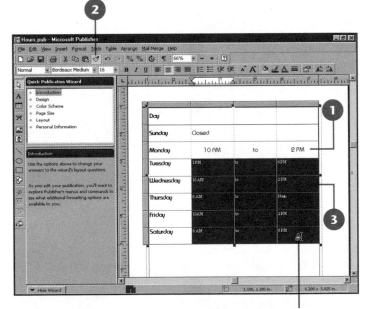

Format Painter pointer

Inserting Rows and Columns

As you work on a table, you may need to modify its structure. For example, you may discover you need another column in the middle of the table for more information, or a row at the top of the table for column titles. When you insert new rows or columns, Publisher adds empty rows or columns with the same formatting and size as the selected one.

TIP

Add a new bottom row.
You can insert a new row at the end of a table as you enter data. Press Tab in the rightmost cell in a row. The insertion point moves to the first cell in the new row.

TIP

Insert rows or columns quickly. *Select one or more entire rows or columns, click the Table menu, and then click Insert Rows or Insert Columns to insert the same number of empty rows or columns below or to the right of the selection.*

Insert a Row or Column

1. Click anywhere in the row or column next to where you want to insert an empty row or column.

2. Click the Table menu, and then click Insert Rows Or Columns.

3. Click the Rows or Columns option button.

4. Enter the number of rows or columns you want to insert.

5. Click the Before Selected Cells or After Selected Cells option button.

6. If you want, click Apply to preview the change.

7. Click OK.

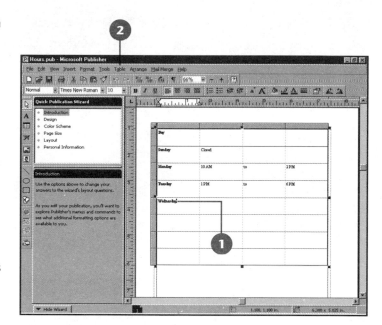

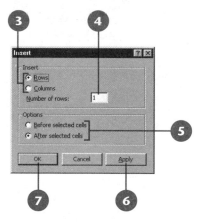

9

Deleting Rows or Columns

If you find that you need to replace the contents of cells in a specific row or column, you can delete the cells' contents without affecting the table frame, while leaving the row or column structure intact. If you find that your table has extra rows or columns you just don't need, you can remove the row or column structure and the cells' contents at the same time. Or, if you decide that you really don't want a table at all, you can delete the entire table quickly.

TIP

Missing commands? *If you don't see the Delete Rows or Delete Columns command on the Table menu, then you probably didn't select the entire row or column. Make sure you click the row or column selection button.*

Delete Cell's Contents

1 Select the cells, rows, or columns whose contents you want to delete.

2 Press Delete.

3 Click in the table to deselect the cells.

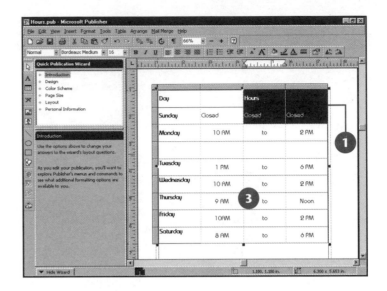

Delete a Row or Column

1 Select the row(s) or column(s) you want to remove.

2 Click the Table menu, and then click Delete Rows or Delete Columns.

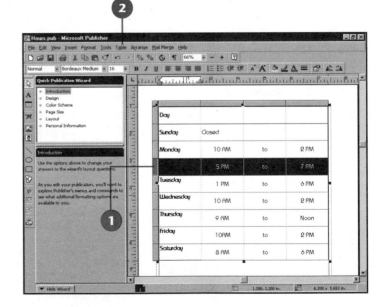

TIP

Format table cells. *You can add lines, border, fill colors and patterns to table cells the same way you add them to text frames. Select one or more cells you want to format with a border or color, and then click the appropriate buttons on the Formatting toolbar.*

TIP

Delete a table's text. *You can quickly delete all the text in a table by selecting the table, right-clicking the selected table, and then clicking Delete Text.*

TIP

Undo a deletion. *If you delete a column, row, or entire table and then change your mind right away, you can quickly retrieve the item. Click the Undo button on the Standard toolbar to restore the deleted row, column, or table.*

TIP

Deleting vs. cutting. *Deleting removes the selection from the table. Cutting removes the selection and places it on the Clipboard so you can paste it into a new location.*

Delete a Table

1 Click in the table you want to delete.

2 Right click the table, and click Delete Object on the shortcut menu.

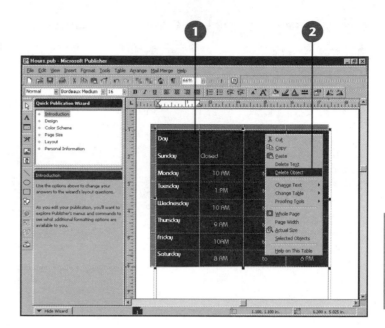

Copying and Moving a Cell's Contents

As you enter text and data into a table, you might find that the data you just entered actually belongs in a different cell or table entirely. You can duplicate that information in another cell or table, or you can move the information there. Either method places the information on the Clipboard, a temporary storage area. Then you can paste the selection from the Clipboard to a new location one or more times.

TIP

Paste over a selection. *To replace existing text with the Clipboard selection, highlight the cells before you paste.*

TIP

Copy and paste shortcuts. *Press Ctrl+C to copy, Ctrl+X to cut, and Ctrl+V to paste.*

Copy a Cell's Contents

1. Select the cell whose contents you want to copy, or select the text in the cell you want to copy.

2. Click the Copy button on the Standard toolbar.

3. Click the cell where you want the text to appear.

4. Click the Paste button on the Standard toolbar.

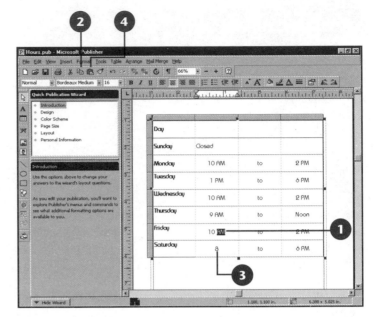

Move a Cell's Contents

1. Select the cell whose contents you want to move, or select the text in the cell you want to move.

2. Click the Cut button on the Standard toolbar.

3. Click the cell where you want the text to appear.

4. Click the Paste button on the Standard toolbar.

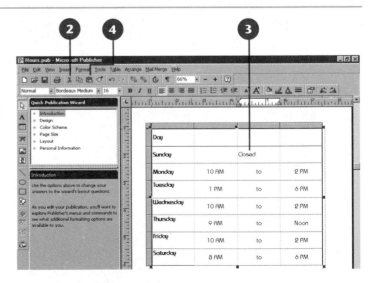

Adjusting Cell Margins

You can change a cell's *margins*—the amount of white space that appears between each edge of a cell and its contents. You can adjust the margins of one cell, a range, or the entire table at once. Unless you lock a table, its size may increase to display all the text within the new margins. The top, bottom, left, and right cell margins can have different measurements, which can be inches (in), centimeters (cm), picas (pi) or points (pt). Cell margins differ from page margins.

TIP

Disappearing table text? *If the table is locked, the margin changes might have blocked some text from view. Click the Table menu, and then click Grow To Fit Text to unlock the table, or make the text size smaller, or resize the table's columns and rows.*

Adjust Cell Margins

1. Select the cell, range, or table whose margins you want to adjust.

2. Click the Table Cell Properties button on the Standard toolbar.

3. Enter the left, right, top, and bottom margin values you want to use.

4. Click OK.

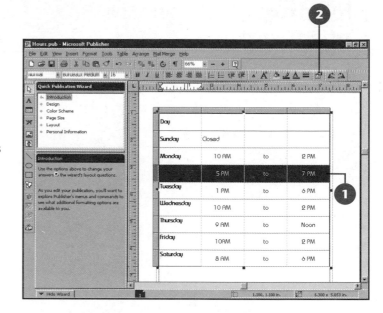

Merging Cells

Tables often display a title spread across the top of the table. If the title is longer than the width of one cell, you can *merge* (combine) cells to form one long cell. In fact, you can merge any block of cells (or even entire rows or columns) as long as they are in adjacent rows or columns. If the cells you merge already contain text, all the text appears in the merged cell. Later you can *split* (or divide) the merged cells back into their original structure. Be aware that all the text in the merged cell is placed in the first split cell.

Merge Cells

1. Select the cells you want to merge.

2. Click the Table menu, and then click Merge Cells.

3. Enter and format text in the cell as usual.

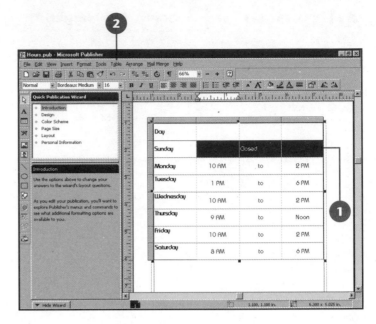

Split Merged Cells

1. Click in the merged cell you want to split.

2. Click the Table menu, and then click Split Cells.

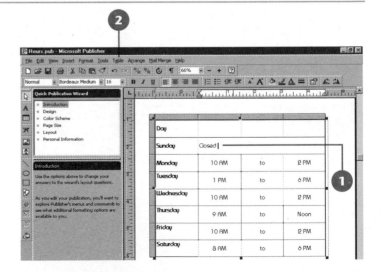

Drawing Diagonal Lines Within Cells

What if you need a column header and row header in the same cell? Instead of choosing one or the other, divide the cell in half diagonally by adding a line that extends from either the upper-left corner to the lower-right corner or from the upper-right corner to the lower-left corner. Use cell diagonals to block out a cell, draw attention to a section, or create an unusual pattern. After you draw the diagonal, enter text in and format each half of the cell as usual. If you remove the diagonal, any text in either half of the cell appears in the undivided cell.

Draw a diagonal line

1. Select the cells you want to divide diagonally.

2. Click the Table menu, and then click Cell Diagonals.

3. Click the Divide Down or Divide Up option button.

4. Click OK.

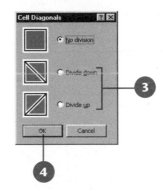

Remove a diagonal line

1. Select the cells you want to remove the diagonal line from.

2. Click the Table menu, and then click Cell Diagonals.

3. Click the No Division option button.

4. Click OK.

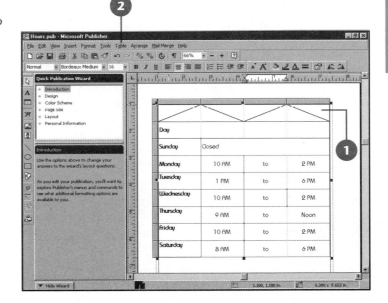

Resizing Tables

You can enlarge or reduce any column width or row height to better display its contents. If you unlock the table, Publisher does this for you. To do this manually, drag the *row boundary* below the row you want to size and *column boundary* to the right of the column you want to resize. After the table text is positioned attractively, you can resize entire table at once. For example, you might reduce a table's size to keep a flyer to one page. When you click in a table, selection handles surround it. Drag a corner handle to resize both the height and width at once. Drag a top, bottom, or side handle to stretch either the table's height or width.

Resize a Table Row or Column

1 Click in the table.

2 Position the mouse pointer over the row boundary below the row you want to resize or the column boundary to the right of the column you want to resize.

3 Drag the boundary to a new position.

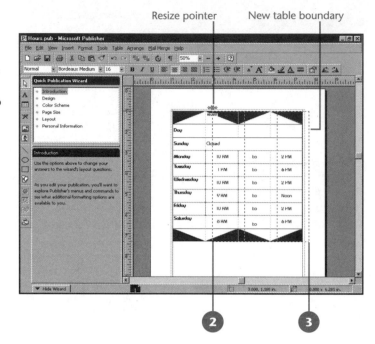

Resize pointer   New table boundary

Resize an Entire Table

1. Click in the table you want to resize.

2. Position the mouse pointer over a resizing handle.

3. Press and hold the Shift key to resize the table proportionally.

4. Drag the resizing handle to a new location.

5. Release the mouse button.

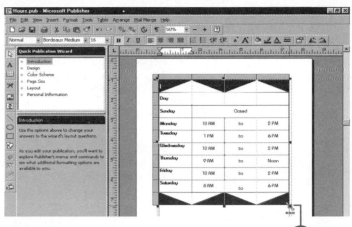

Resize pointer on corner handle 2

Move a Table

1. Click in the table you want to move.

2. Position the mouse pointer over any edge of the table frame until you see the move pointer.

3. Drag the table to a new position.

4. Release the mouse button.

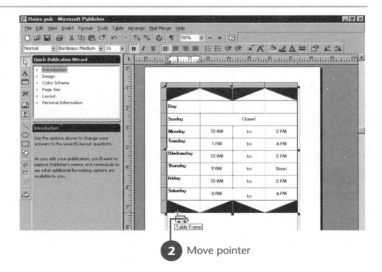

2 Move pointer

9

Importing a Table

Many times the information you want already exists in another document. Rather than retype the information, risking errors, you can *import* (or insert) it into a publication. You can copy and paste data from an existing table or worksheet cells from Word, Excel, or another Windows-based program. You can also import paragraphs of text and then have Publisher create a table from them. You need only to make sure a tab character separates the information for each column and a paragraph mark separates the information for each row.

Import a Table from Word or Excel

1. Open a worksheet or document with a table.

2. Select the cells to import.

3. Click the Copy button on the Standard toolbar.

4. Open the publication.

5. Click the Paste button on the Standard toolbar.

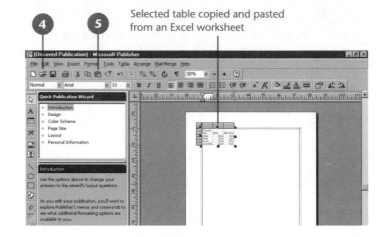

Selected table copied and pasted from an Excel worksheet

Create a Table from Imported Text

1. Open the document with the text you want to use.

2. Press Tab between each column's data and press the Enter key at the end of each row, if necessary.

3. Select the text.

4. Click the Copy button on the Standard toolbar.

5. Open the publication.

6. Click the Edit menu, and then click Paste Special.

7. Double-click New Table.

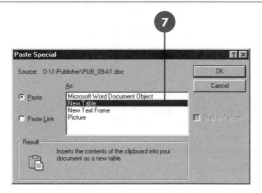

Creating Custom Publications

Microsoft Publisher 2000 comes with a variety of features that enable you to work efficiently and more comfortably. Tools, such as templates and personal information sets that contain data and formatting you reuse, make the creation of repetitive publications quick and easy.

Customizing Your Workspace

As you become more familiar with Publisher, you'll find many tools that make your work environment more comfortable and efficient. You can customize the location and appearance of toolbars, and reposition and resize them to suit your needs. Smart objects—Design Gallery objects with wizards—are easy to insert, and can be modified easily. Any changes to a smart object are updated throughout a publication. You can add any objects to the Design Gallery so they'll always be available for your use. Modify personal information that you use repeatedly throughout your publications. It, too, is also updated throughout a publication whenever changes are made. As you work with Publisher, menus and toolbars conform to your work habits. If you choose, you can revert back to the original settings.

Creating a Quick Publication

Occasionally you'll want to create a one-page publication that does not fit into any of the categories listed in Publisher's Catalog—for example, a title page for a report. When you want to create a page quickly, use the Quick Publications Wizard. After Publisher creates a page based on your selection, you can use the list of wizard options as a guide for customizing the page.

TIP

Step through the wizard.
You can have the wizard ask you a series of questions about your formatting and design options. These questions correspond to the categories you see in the wizard area of the Publisher window. Click the Tools menu, click Options, click the User Assistance tab, click to select the Step Through Wizard Questions check box, and then click OK.

Create a New Quick Publication

1 In the Catalog dialog box, click the Publications By Wizard tab.

2 Click Quick Publications.

3 Click the thumbnail that displays the design for the publication you want.

4 Click Start Wizard.

5 Answer the wizard questions as you step through them.

Click Next to continue or click Back to review your answers.

6 When you're done, click Finish.

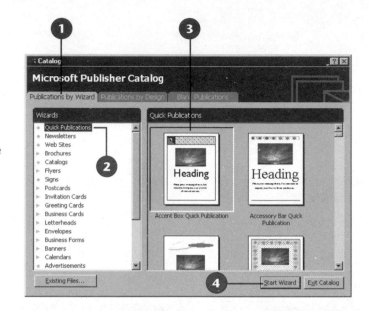

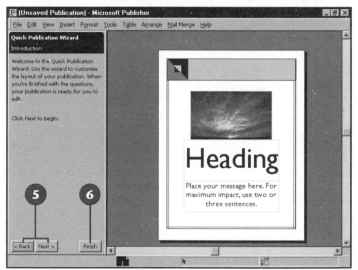

Creating a Publication By Design

You can create a publication based on the type of design you want. If you want to create a consistent look for your business cards, calendars, letterhead, and so on, use the Publication By Design feature.

TIP

Bypass wizard questions without changing user assistance options. *Click the Finish button in the wizard window to complete the wizard without stepping through the remaining questions. Publisher creates your publication using default settings.*

Create a New Publication By Design

1. In the Catalog dialog box, click the Publications By Design tab.

2. Click a design set, and then click a specific design.

3. Click the thumbnail that represents the kind of publication you want to create.

4. Click Start Wizard.

5. Answer the wizard questions as you step through them for design, color scheme, orientation, logo, printing, and other options.

   Click Next to continue or click Back to review your answers.

6. When you're done, click Finish.

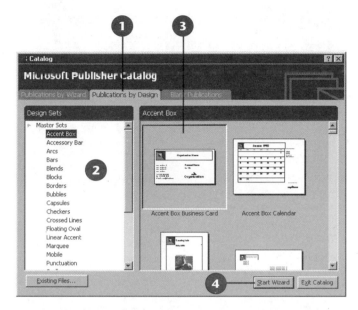

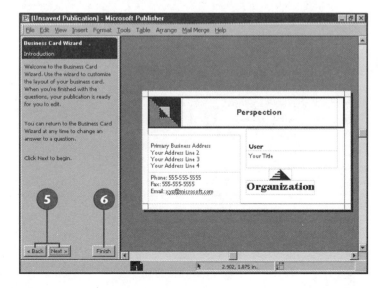

Creating Letterhead

Well-designed letterhead communicates as much as the content of your letter. In fact, your message can be easily overlooked or contradicted by visually boring or poorly designed letterhead. Letterhead you create in Publisher combines attractive design elements that enhance, but don't detract from the content of your letter. To convey a serious message, choose a formal design, like Bars or Crossed Lines. For a more creative feel, choose the innovative or visually exciting Waves or Bubbles. Individuals in technical fields often prefer the clean, austere look of Punctuation or Linear Accent. Of course, the final decision is yours, but when choosing a letterhead design, be sure to consider the content of letter, the recipient, and amount of information you want to present.

Create a Letterhead Without Stepping Through the Wizard

1 Click the Tools menu, click Options, click the User Assistance tab, click to clear the Step through Wizard Questions check box, and then click OK.

2 In the Catalog dialog box, click the Publications By Wizard tab.

3 Click Letterheads.

4 Click Plain Paper or Special Paper.

5 Double-click the thumbnail that displays the design you want for your letterhead.

Publisher creates a letterhead.

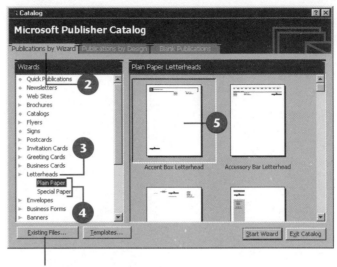

Click to open existing publications.

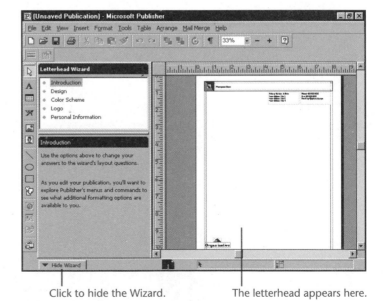

Click to hide the Wizard.

The letterhead appears here.

Turn on Step Through Wizard Questions feature. *Click the Tools menu, click Options, click the User Assistance tab, click to select the Step Through Wizard Questions check box, and then click OK.*

Test your printer. *If you do not have a color printer, test different color schemes to see how specific colors appear when you print on a black and white printer.*

Change your mind when stepping through a wizard. *Click the Back button to return to a previous wizard question and make different selections.*

Step Through a Wizard to Create Letterhead

1. In the Catalog dialog box, click the Publications By Wizard tab.

2. Click Letterheads, and then click Plain Paper or Special Paper.

3. Double-click the thumbnail that displays the design for your letterhead.

4. Click Next to continue.

5. From the palette, click a color scheme for your letterhead, and then click Next to continue.

6. Click Yes if you want to use a logo, and then click Next to continue.

7. Click the name and address information that you want to appear.

8. Click Finish.

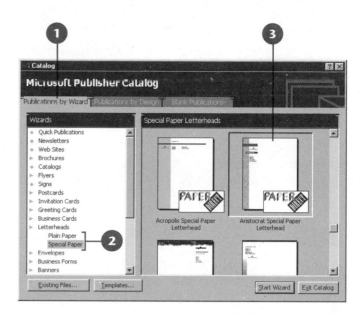

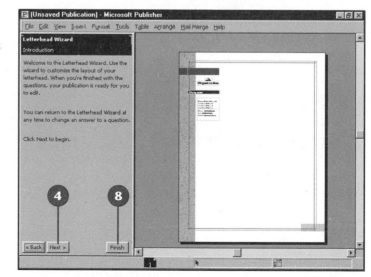

Creating a Business Card

A business card is a small but important publication that communicates volumes about you and your line of work. A business card you create with Publisher not only provides the essentials (your name, company name, address, and phone numbers), but also informs the recipient that you are a capable, efficient person (especially if you include your e-mail address, fax, and cell phone numbers) with flair for good design and eye for the aesthetic.

TRY THIS

Create a personal business card. *You don't have to be a businessperson to use a business card. The Business Card Wizard allows you to create a business card that contains personal (rather than professional) information.*

Create a Business Card

1. In the Catalog dialog box, click the Publications By Wizard tab.

2. Click Business Cards.

3. Click Plain Paper or Special Paper.

4. Click the thumbnail that displays the design of business card you want to create.

5. Click Start Wizard.

6. Answer each question as you step through the wizard.

Publisher creates a business card based on the registration information stored in the User Info dialog box.

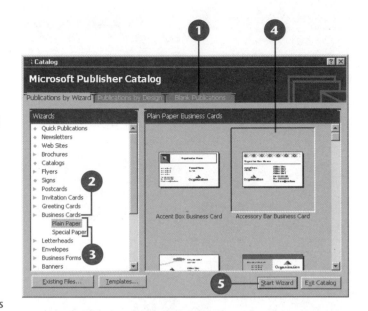

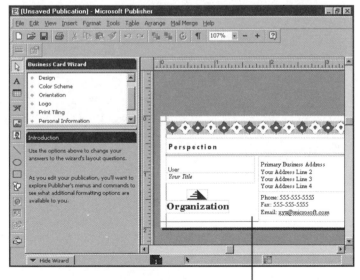

The business card appears here.

Creating a Brochure

A brochure is a publication that can address multiple communications needs. You can describe your products and services, include text and images, and provide forms for placing orders, getting information, or signing up for something. Publisher brochures provide areas for information on the front and back of several panels (3 panels if you are using 8.5-by-11-inch paper, 4 panels if you are using legal size paper). And you can even mail it to customers without using an envelope.

TIP

Switch between pages. *You can see information on the other pages of a publication by clicking the page thumbnail in the status bar at the bottom of the window. Each thumbnail corresponds to a page in your publication.*

Create a Brochure

1. In the Catalog dialog box, click the Publications By Wizard tab.

2. Click Brochures.

3. Click one of the brochure categories

4. Double-click the thumbnail that displays the design for your brochure.

5. Click Next to continue.

6. Click a color scheme for your brochure, and then click Next.

7. Indicate the size of paper you'll use to print the brochure, and then click Next.

8. Choose if you want to include a customer address, and then click Next.

9. Choose a form (if any) that you want to appear on page two, and then click Next to continue.

10. Choose the name and address information that you want to appear.

11. Click Finish to create a brochure based on your responses to the wizard.

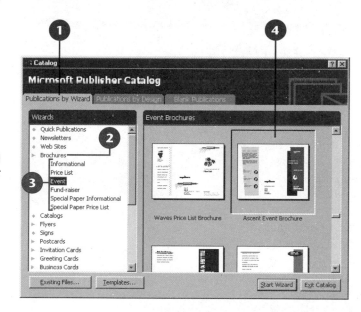

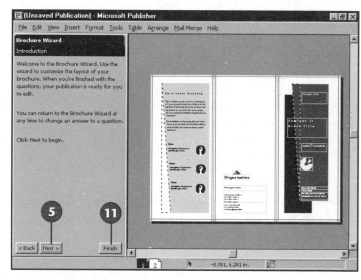

10

Creating a Newsletter

A newsletter is a great way to communicate information on a regular basis. Businesses can use newsletters to inform customers about new products and services, answer frequently asked customer support questions, or generate interest in upcoming events. For personal use, you can distribute a newsletter to update family members on family matters or use a newsletter as a creative alternative to the typical holiday letter. Using the Newsletter Wizard in Publisher, you can create a multiple page newsletter formatted with one, two, three, or a combination of columns. You can also include forms, calendars, and other inside pages formatted for text and graphics. After you create the newsletter, use additional wizards to create inside pages and insert new pages.

Step Through a Wizard to Create Newsletter

1. In the Catalog, click the Publications By Wizard tab.

2. Click Newsletters.

3. Double-click the thumbnail that displays the design for your newsletter.

4. Click Next to continue.

5. Choose a color scheme for your newsletter, and then click Next to continue.

6. Indicate the number of columns you want, and then click Next to continue.

7. Click Yes if you want to allow space for a customer address, and then click Next to continue.

8. Indicate whether you want one-sided or two-sided printing, and then click Next to continue.

9. Choose the name and address information that you want to appear.

10. Click Finish to create a newsletter based on your responses to the wizard.

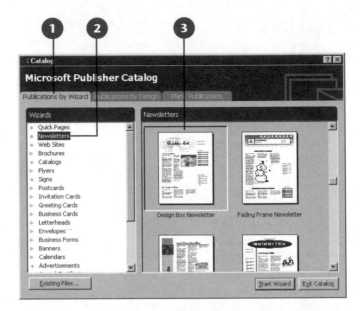

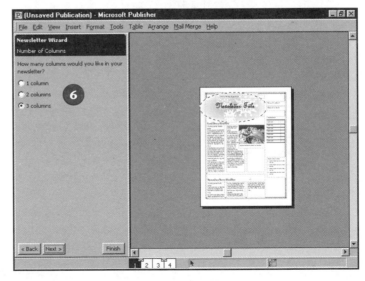

TIP

Convert your newsletter to a Web page. *Reuse the information in a newsletter on your Web site. Click the Convert To Web Site option in the wizard area of the window. This option starts the Web Site Wizard.*

TIP

An option preceded by the symbol xxx in a wizard is not available. *If you click an option that is not available, a message appears telling you what you need to do to use that option.*

TRY THIS

Insert multiple pages in your newsletter. *In the Insert Page dialog box, click the More Options button. Then you can select the number of pages to insert, where to insert them, and the content to include on all the new pages.*

Use the Wizard to Create Inside Pages in a Newsletter

1. In the status bar, click the number of an inside page.

2. Click Inside Page Content.

3. In the bottom panel, click the drop-down arrow and choose the page for the new content.

4. Click the content option to include on this page.

5. Repeat steps 2 and 3 for each inside page.

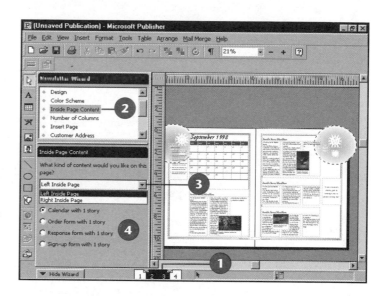

Use the Wizard to Insert a Page in a Newsletter

1. In the status bar, click the number of an inside page.

2. Click the Insert Page option.

3. Click Insert Page.

4. Click the drop-down arrow, and then select a content option for this page.

5. Click OK.

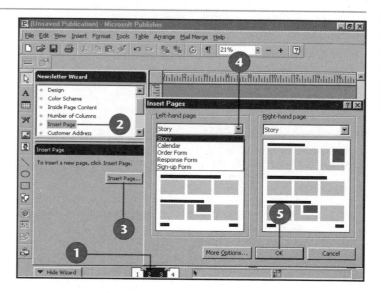

10

Using Templates

As you work with Publisher, you may find that you use a particular publication again and again. Perhaps you prepare a newsletter using the same format each month. You can save a model publication, or *template*, with text, graphics, and ruler and layout guides that you can later reuse.

TIP

No Templates button. *The Template button only appears if you have templates in the Catalog.*

TIP

Unsaved templates. *When you open a template, its name is "Unsaved"—just like opening a blank publication. This feature means your template will never be changed. No matter how many times it's opened, you always have a fresh copy.*

Apply a Template

1. Click the File menu, and then click New.

2. Click Templates.

3. Double-click the template you want to use.

4. If necessary, make any changes to your publication.

5. Click the File menu, and then click Save.

6. Select the drive and folder in which to store the publication.

7. Type a name for the file.

8. Click Save.

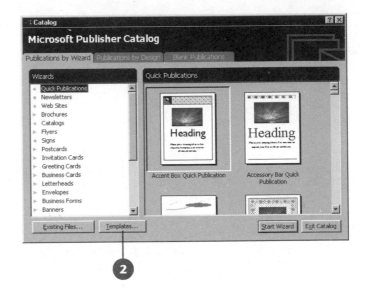

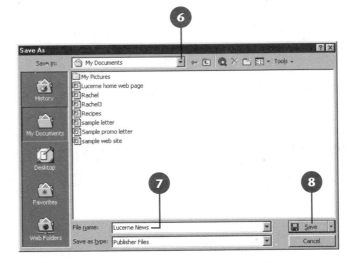

Save a Publication as a Template

1. Click the File menu, and then click Save As.

2. Select the drive and folder in which to store the template.

3. Type a name for the template.

4. Click the Save As Type drop-down arrow, and then click Publisher Template.

5. Click Save.

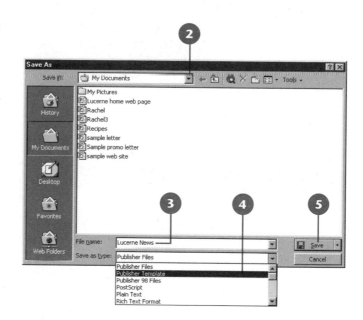

Creating Personal Information Sets

Each time you create a publication, you probably use the same information about yourself or your business. Instead of having to enter this information each time, Publisher stores this data in one of four personal information sets. Each set includes eight components: personal name, job title, organization name, address, tag line, phone, fax, e-mail, logo, and color scheme. You can change or delete the information in any set.

TIP

Default personal information set. *The Primary Business Personal Information Set is the default selection for each new publication.*

Select a Personal Information Set in a Wizard

1. Click the File menu, and then click New.

2. Select a wizard, and then double-click a thumbnail.

3. Answer the wizard questions as you step through the wizard.

4. Click a Personal Information Set option button.

5. Click Finish.

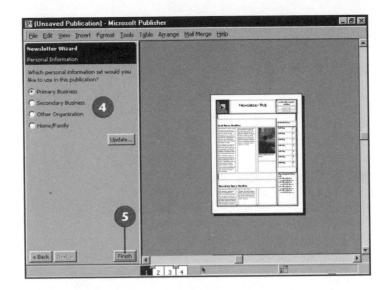

Insert a Personal Information Component

1. Click the Insert menu, and then point to Personal Information.

2. Click a Personal Information Component from the menu.

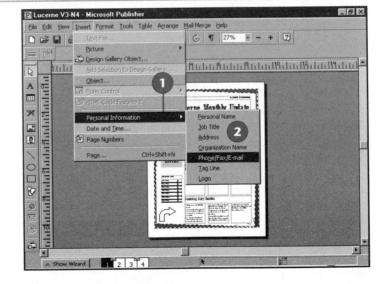

TIP

Updated personal Information. *Changes made to a personal information set are updated throughout the current publication.*

TIP

Make sure synchronization is turned on. *If you modify a personal information set and the change is not reflected elsewhere in a publication, synchronization may be turned off.*

TRY THIS

Modify a personal information component. *Make a change to a personal information component with multiple occurrences in a publication. Verify that the information changed in each occurrence.*

SEE ALSO

See "Ensuring Consistency with Synchronization" on page 117 for information on turning this feature on and off.

Edit a Personal Information Set

1. Click the Edit menu, and then click Personal Information.

2. Click an information set from the Choose A Personal Information Set To Edit list.

3. Make changes in the Personal Information Set.

4. Click Update.

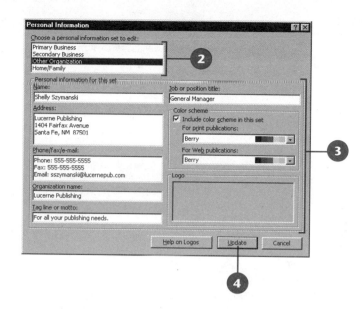

Remove a Personal Information Component

1. Click the Edit menu, and then click Personal Information.

2. Click an information set from the Choose A Personal Information Set To Edit list.

3. Delete any information you want removed.

4. Click Update.

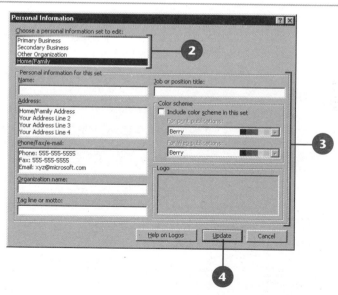

10

Using Smart Objects

You'll find that some objects created using the Design Gallery—logos, ads, calendars, or coupons—include a wizard button. This wizard button indicates a *smart object* that you can modify. When you modify a smart object, Publisher updates each occurrence of the object in the current publication. Many publications created using the Catalog also contain smart objects. Use the synchronization feature so each occurrence of a smart object is identical.

TIP

Reverse smart object changes. *If you don't like the results of changes you've made to a smart object, click the Undo button on the Standard toolbar.*

SEE ALSO

See "Ensuring Consistency with Synchronization" on page 117 for information on turning this feature on and off.

Insert a Smart Object

1. Click the Design Gallery Object button on the Objects toolbar.

2. Click a smart object category: logos, advertisements, coupons, or calendars, for example.

3. Click the thumbnail.

4. Click Insert Object.

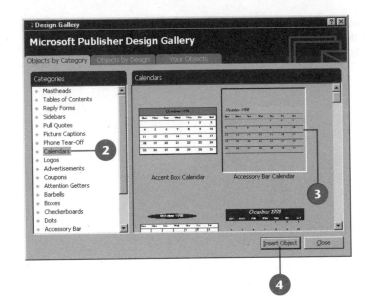

Change a Smart Object Design

1. Click the smart object's wizard button.

2. Click an option in the wizard's upper window.

3. Click an option in the wizard's lower window.

4. Click the Close button on the wizard.

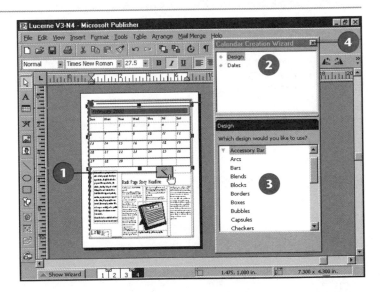

Add an Object to the Design Gallery

1. Click the object(s) you want to add to the Design Gallery.

2. Click the Insert menu, and then click Add Selection To Design Gallery.

3. Type a name for the object.

4. Make a selection from the Category list, or type the name of a new category.

5. Click OK.

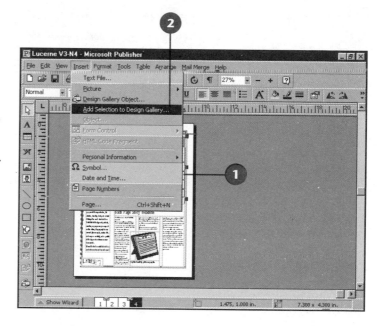

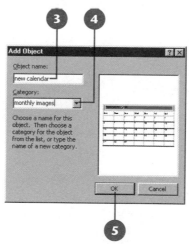

10

Creating a Personal Logo

A logo is an easily identifiable symbol associated with a person, business, or organization. Publisher makes it easy to create a logo using the Design Gallery's Logo Creation Wizard. A logo can contain text, a graphic image, or both, and can be added to any of the four personal information sets. For example, you can add your company's logo to a personal information set that appears in all newsletters or brochures.

SEE ALSO

See "Using Smart Objects" on page 168 for information on how smart objects are automatically updated.

SEE ALSO

See "Creating Personal Information Sets" on page 166 for instructions on storing four different information profiles.

Create a Logo

1. Click the Design Gallery Object button on the Objects toolbar.

2. Click the Objects By Category tab.

3. Click Logos.

4. Double-click a logo thumbnail.

5. If necessary, select and replace text.

6. If necessary, click the Smart Object Wizard button, and then make any design changes.

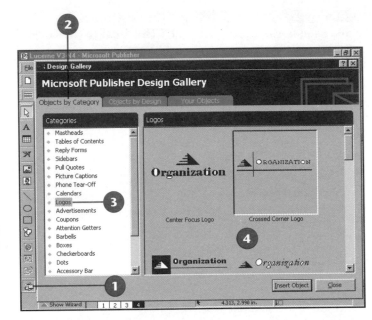

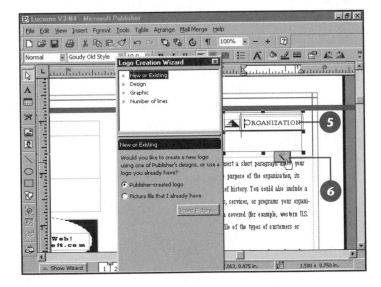

Modifying Your Design Gallery

The Design Gallery contains a large collection of objects you can use to enhance your publications. You can also store your own unique objects on the Design Gallery's Your Objects tab. This means that once you create an object, you can store it in the Design Gallery for use at any time.

When you initially create a publication, the Your Objects tab is empty. You can add objects—and create your own categories—within the Your Objects tab. You can also remove or rename objects and their categories.

SEE ALSO

See "Using Smart Objects" on page 168 for information on inserting an object into the Design Gallery.

Rename an Object

1. Click the Design Gallery Object button on the Objects toolbar.

2. Click the Your Objects tab.

3. Click the category containing the object you want to rename.

4. Right-click an object's thumbnail, and then click Rename This Object.

5. Type the new name in the To box.

6. Click OK.

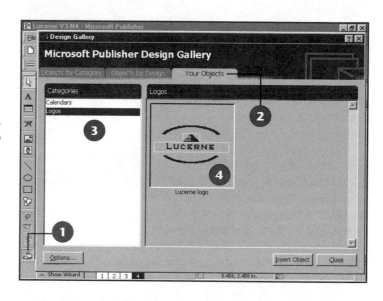

Remove an Object

1. Click the Design Gallery Object button on the Objects toolbar.

2. Click the Your Objects tab.

3. Click the category containing the object you want to remove.

4. Right-click an object's thumbnail, and then click Delete This Object.

5. Click Yes.

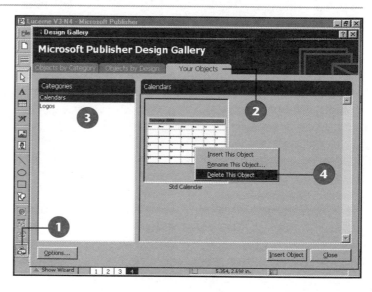

10

Customizing Toolbars

Publisher gives you the flexibility to rearrange toolbars so you can work efficiently with the tools you need. Frequently used, but not visible buttons are available on both the Standard and Formatting toolbars by clicking the More Buttons drop-down arrow.

Toolbars can float anywhere in the Publisher window, or can "dock" along any edge. When you drag a floating toolbar to an edge, you'll see it "snap" into place. You can resize a floating toolbar by clicking and dragging an edge, just like any window.

TIP

Display the More Buttons button. *This button is only displayed if there are additional buttons that don't fit on a toolbar.*

Display More Buttons

1. Click the More Buttons drop-down arrow.

2. Click a button on the palette.

Move a Toolbar

1. If the toolbar is docked, click the move handle.

   If the toolbar is floating, click the title bar.

2. Drag the toolbar to a new location.

Drag a toolbar's title bar to move the tollbar.

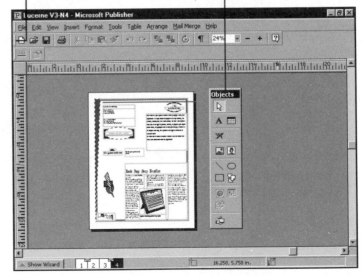

Display a Toolbar

1. Right-click anywhere on any toolbar.

2. Click the toolbar you want to display or hide.

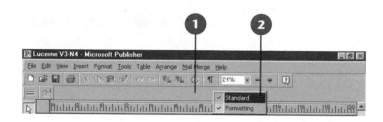

Change the Size of Toolbar Buttons

1. Right-click the workspace, and then point to Toolbars.

2. Click Options.

3. Click to select or clear the Large Icons check box.

   If the check box is selected, toolbar buttons appear larger than if the check box is cleared.

4. Click OK.

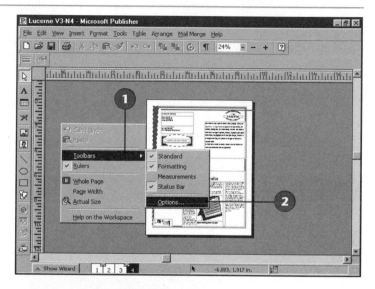

Changing Usage Settings

You can return Publisher to its default appearance by resetting the usage settings. You may have noticed that when you initially look for a command, it may not be on the menu. Then—after a few seconds—it appears. Once you've used a "hidden" command, it does appear on the menu. These *intelligent menus* adjust their appearances to your work habits. The same is true for toolbar buttons that don't appear until you use the More Buttons button.

Change Usage Settings

1. Click the Tools menu, and then click Options.

2. Click the General tab.

3. Click Reset Usage Data.

4. Click OK.

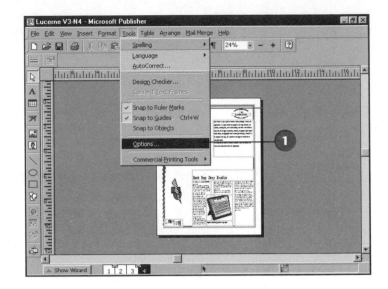

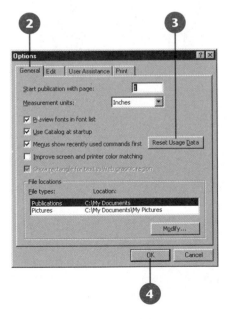

**Turn off the Intelligent
Menus feature.** *If you want
to always see all menu commands, click the Tools menu,
click Options, and then click the
General tab. Click to clear the
Make sure the Menus Show
Recently Used Commands First
check box, and then click OK.*

Change General Settings

1. Click the Tools menu, and then click Options.

2. Click the General tab.

3. Click to select or clear the settings you want.

4. Click OK.

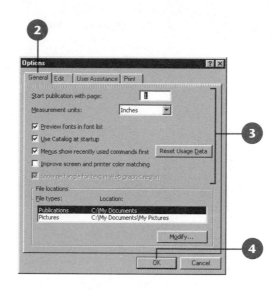

**Change the default Open
and Save file location.** *Click
the Tools menu, click Options,
and then click the General tab.
Click Publications in the File
Locations box, click Modify,
select a folder location, and
then click OK.*

Change User Assistance Settings

1. Click the Tools menu, and then click Options.

2. Click the User Assistance tab.

3. Click to select or clear the settings you want.

4. Click OK.

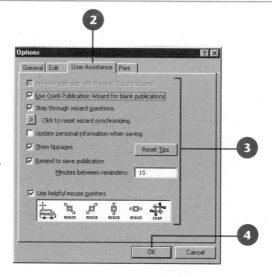

10

Changing Your View

You can view the pages in your publication in various magnification levels. Viewing the page at a reduced size allows you to see an overview of your design. Zooming in on the pages makes type legible and provides a higher degree of accuracy when creating or positioning frames.

TIP

Switch between two different view sizes. *Press F9 key to toggle back and forth between actual size (100%) and the current view size.*

TIP

Zoom and scroll using Microsoft IntelliMouse. *Roll the wheel to scroll, or press and hold Ctrl and roll the wheel to zoom.*

Change the View Size of a Page

1. Click the Zoom drop-down arrow on the Standard toolbar.

2. Select the view percentage you want.

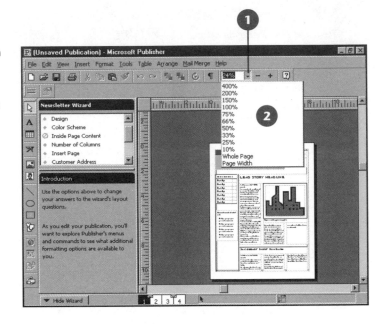

Working with Other Programs

Microsoft Office 2000 has the power and flexibility to share information between programs. This means you can create, store, and manage information in the program that works best for that type of information, and move that same information to another program for a specific purpose or presentation.

Share with Ease

Consider an example. Sarah coordinates her local school district's soccer teams. She sends out monthly newsletters that list the scheduled dates and times for practices and games as well as a brief roundup of scores and highlights from the previous month's games. In Microsoft Excel, she creates a list of team members and all their relevant information—names, addresses, phone numbers, emergency numbers, and team positions. She also tracks the year-to-date expenses and plans the tentative schedules between teams. Every month, Sarah writes the newsletter in Microsoft Publisher 2000, imports the upcoming schedule from Excel, and then merges the newsletter with the Excel worksheet to create the mailing. This is just one scenario. As you work with Publisher and other Office programs, you'll find many ways to share information between them.

Sharing Information Between Programs

All Office 2000 programs, including Publisher, can convert data or text from one format to another using a technology known as *object linking and embedding (OLE)*. OLE allows you to move text or data between programs in much the same way as you move them within a program. The familiar cut and paste or drag-and-drop methods work between programs and documents just as they do within a document. In addition, all Office programs have special ways to move information from one program to another, including importing, exporting, embedding, linking, and hyperlinking.

Importing and Exporting

Importing and exporting information are two sides of the same coin. *Importing* copies a file created with the same or another program into your open file. The information becomes part of your open file, just as if you created it in that format, although formatting and program-specific information such as formulas can be lost. *Exporting* converts a copy of your open file into the file type of another program. In other words, importing brings information into your open document, while exporting moves information from your open document into another program file.

Embedding

Embedding inserts a copy of a file created in one program into a file created in another program. Unlike imported files, you can edit the information in embedded files with the same commands and toolbar buttons used to create the original file. The original file is called the *source file*, while the file in which it is embedded is called the *destination file*. Any changes you make to an embedded object appear only in the destination file; the source file remains unchanged.

Linking

Linking displays information from one file (the source file) in a file created in another program (the destination file). You can view and edit the linked object from either the source file or the destination file. The changes are stored in the source file but also appear in the destination file. As you work, Office updates the linked object to ensure you always have the most current information. Office keeps track of all the drive, folder, and filename information for a source file. However, if you move or rename the source file, the link between files will break.

Once the link is broken, the information in the destination file becomes embedded rather than linked. In other words, changes to one copy of the file will no longer affect the other.

TERM	DEFINITION
Source program	The program that created the original object
Source file	The file that contains the original object
Destination program	The program that created the document into which you are inserting the object
Destination file	The file into which you are inserting the object

Hyperlinking

The newest way to share information between programs is hyperlinks—a term borrowed from World Wide Web technology. A *hyperlink* is an object (either colored, underlined text or a graphic) that you click to jump to a different location in the same document or a different document. (See "Adding a Hyperlink" on page 196 for more information about creating and navigating hyperlinks in Publisher documents.)

Deciding Which Method to Use

With of all theses different methods for sharing information between programs to choose from, sometimes it is hard to decide which method to use. To decide which method is best for your situation, answer the following questions.

1 Do you want the contents of another file displayed in the open document?

- ◆ **No**. Create a hyperlink. See "Adding a Hyperlink" on page 196.
- ◆ **Yes**. Go to question 2.

2 Do you want to edit the content of the file from within the open document?

- ◆ **No**. Embed the file as a picture. See "Inserting a Picture" on page 86.
- ◆ **Yes**. Go to question 3.

3 Is the source program (the program used to create the file) available on your computer?

- ◆ **No**. Import the file. See "Importing and Exporting Files" on page 180.
- ◆ **Yes**. Go to question 4.

4 Do you want to use the source program commands to edit the file?

- ◆ **No**. Import the file. See "Importing and Exporting Files" on page 180.
- ◆ **Yes**. Go to question 5.

5 Do you want changes you make to the file to appear in the source file (the original copy of the file)?

- ◆ **No**. Embed the file. See "Embedding an Object" on page 182.
- ◆ **Yes**. Link the file. See "Linking an Object" on page 184.

11

Importing and Exporting Files

When you import data, you insert a copy of a file (from the same or another program) into an open publication. When you export data, you save an open document in a new format so that it can be opened in an entirely different program. For example, you might import an Excel worksheet into a Publisher document to create a report with text and a table. Or you might want to export part of an Excel worksheet to use in the corporate newsletter you created in Publisher.

Import a File

1. Click where you want to insert the imported file.

2. Click the Insert menu, and then click Text File.

3. Click the Files Of Type drop-down arrow, and then select All Files.

4. Click the Look In drop-down arrow, and then select the drive and folder of the file you want to import.

5. Double-click the name of the file you want to import.

6. Edit the imported information with the open program's commands.

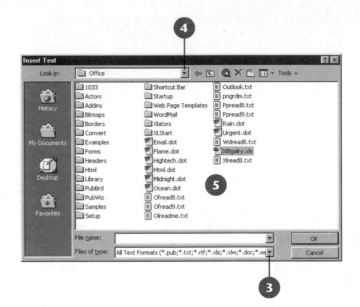

TIP

Use copy and paste to export information. *If you want to move only part of a file into your document, just copy the information you want to insert, and then paste the information in the file where you want it to appear.*

TRY THIS

Share a file with another user. *Export a file to an earlier version of a program or a similar program type so someone else can edit, format, and print it. For example, you might save a Publisher publication as a Word 97 document.*

Export a File to Another Format

1. Click the File menu, and then click Save As.

2. If necessary, click the Save In drop-down arrow, and then select the drive and folder where you want to save the file.

3. Click the Save As Type drop-down arrow, and then select the type of file you want.

4. If necessary, type a new name for the file.

5. Click Save.

   The file is saved in the specified format.

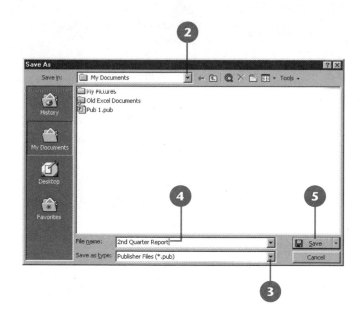

11

Embedding an Object

Embedding inserts a copy of one object into another publication or document. Once data is embedded, you can edit it in the program in which it was created (the source program). The embedded data becomes part of the publication or document (the destination file). You can embed an exisiting or new object.

SEE ALSO

See "Sharing Information Between Programs" on page 178 for more information embedding objects.

TIP

Work with embedded objects. *If you click an embedded object, you simply select it. If you double-click an embedded object, you activate it and the source toolbars and menus appear.*

Embed an Existing Object

1. Click where you want to embed the object.

2. Click the Insert menu, and then click Object.

3. Click the Create From File option button.

4. Click Browse, and then double-click the file with the object you want to embed.

5. Click OK.

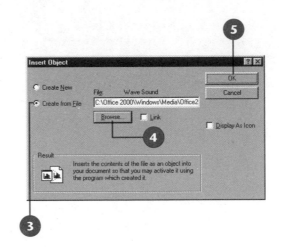

Embed a New Object

1. Click where you want to embed the object.

2. Click the Insert menu, and then click Object.

3. Click the Create New option button.

4. Double-click the type of object you want to create.

5. Enter information in the new object using the source program's commands.

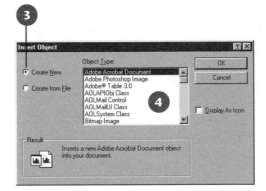

Copy and Paste to Embed an Object

1 Open the program where the object (Excel chart, PowerPoint slide, and so on) you want to use appears.

2 Click to select the object you want to embed.

3 Click the Copy button on the Standard toolbar.

4 Switch to your publication, and then click the publication where you want to embed the object.

5 Click the Paste button on the Standard toolbar.

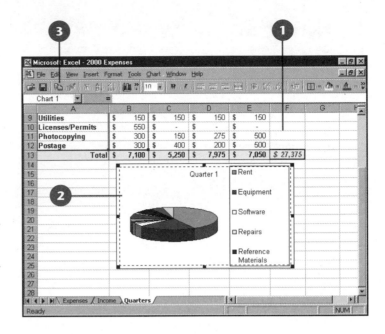

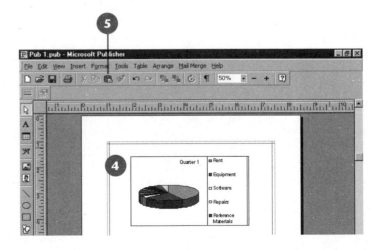

11

Linking an Object

Linking displays information stored in one document (the source file) in another (the destination file). You can edit the linked object from either file, although changes are stored in the source file. For example, you might link an Excel chart to a Publisher document and a Word document so you can update the chart from any of the files.

SEE ALSO

See "Sharing Information Between Programs" on page 178 for more information linking objects.

TIP

Insert objects as icons. *If you insert an object as an icon, you can double-click the icon to view the object.*

Paste Link an Object

1. In the source program, select the object you want to paste link.

2. Click the Cut or Copy button on the Standard toolbar in the source program.

3. Switch to your publication.

4. Click the Edit menu, and then click Paste Special.

5. Click the Paste Link option button.

6. Click the object type you want.

7. Click OK.

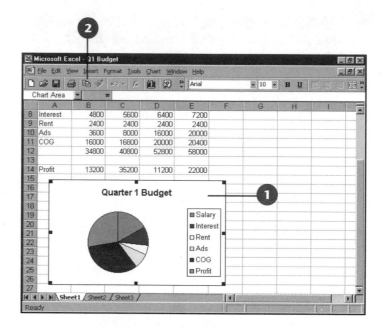

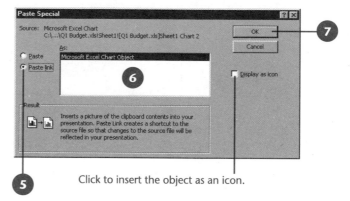

Click to insert the object as an icon.

SEE ALSO

See Section 13, "Using Mail Merge," on page 213 for information on merging address information in a publication to create a mailing list.

SEE ALSO

See "Embedding an Object" on page 182 for information on embedding objects instead of linking objects.

Link an Object Between Programs

1. Click where you want to link the object.

2. Click the Insert menu, and then click Object.

3. Click the Create From File option button.

4. Click Browse, and then double-click the object you want to link.

5. Click to select the Link check box.

6. Click OK.

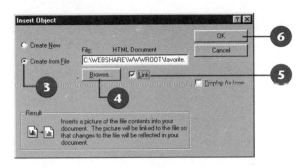

Edit an Embedded or Linked File

1. Double click the linked or embedded object you want to edit to display the source program's menus and toolbars.

2. Edit the object as usual using the source program's commands.

3. When you're done, click outside the object to return to the destination program.

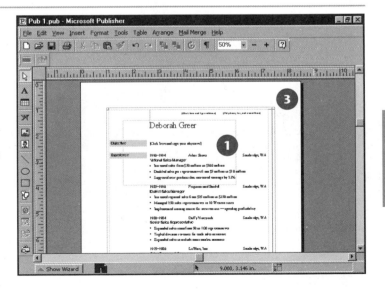

11

Modifying Links

When you modify a linked object, it is usually updated in the destination document. However, you can choose to update the link manually. Publisher gives you control over the links you have established. You can change the source file and you can break a link at any time. You can also convert a linked object to another object type.

Update Links

1. Open the publication that contains the links you want to update.

2. Click the Edit menu, and then click Links.

3. Click the link you want to update.

4. Click Update Now.

5. Click Close.

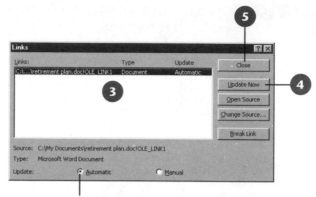

Click so that links will be updated automatically whenever the document is reopened.

Change the Source of a Linked Object

1. Click the Edit menu, and then click Links.

2. Click the link whose source you want to change.

3. Click Change Source.

4. Locate and double-click the new source file.

5. Click Close.

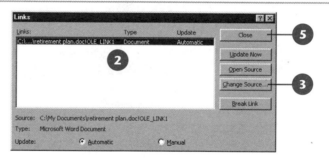

TIP

Edit an embedded object in the source program.
Double-click the embedded object to open it. Make the changes you want to the object. If you edit the object in the open program, click anywhere outside the object to return to the destination file. If you edit the object in the source program, click the File menu, and then click Exit to return to the destination file.

"How can I ensure that changes I make to the source file won't affect the object in my publication?"

Break a Link

1. Click the Edit menu, and then click Links.

2. Click the link you want to break.

3. Click Break Link.

   The link no longer appears in the Links dialog box.

4. Click Close.

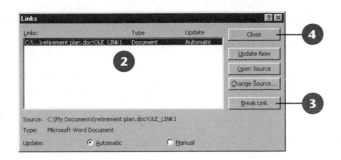

Convert a Linked Object

1. Click the linked object whose file type you want to convert.

2. Click the Edit menu, and then point to Linked Object. This command might appear as Linked Chart Object, or some other file type, depending on the object type.

3. Click Convert.

4. Click the new object type you want.

5. Click OK.

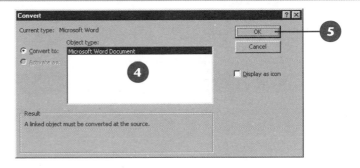

11

Creating a Graph Chart

A chart often makes numerical data more visual and easier to grasp. With Microsoft Graph, you can create a chart in Publisher. Just enter your numbers and labels in the *datasheet*, a spreadsheet-like grid of rows and columns that holds your data in *cells* (intersections of rows and columns), and watch Graph create the *chart*, a graphical representation of the data. Each *data series*, all the data from a row or column, has a unique color or pattern on the chart. You can format *chart objects*, individual elements that make up a chart, such as an axis, legend, or data series, to suit your needs.

Create a Graph Chart

1. Click where you want to insert the chart.

2. Click the Insert menu, click Object, and then double-click Microsoft Graph 2000 Chart.

3. Click the datasheet's upper-left button to select all the cells, and then press Delete to erase the sample data.

4. Enter new data in each cell, or click the Import Data button on the Standard toolbar to insert data from another source, such as an Excel worksheet.

5. Edit and format the data in the datasheet as you like.

6. Click the Close button on the datasheet to close it.

7. Click outside the chart to quit Microsoft Graph and return to your publication.

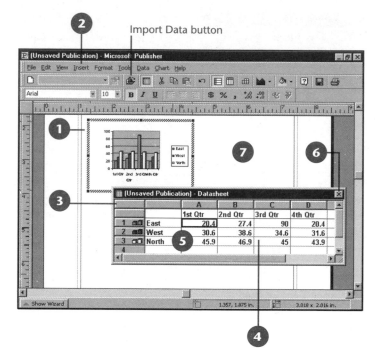

Import Data button

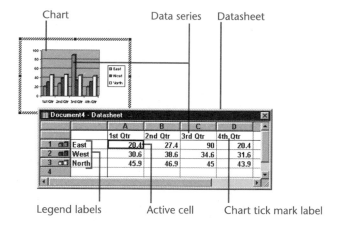

Chart   Data series   Datasheet

Legend labels   Active cell   Chart tick mark label

Format a Chart Object

1. In Graph, double-click the chart object you want to format, such as an axis, legend, or data series.

2. Click the tab (Patterns, Scale, Font, Number, or Alignment) corresponding to the options you want to change.

3. Select the options to apply.

4. Click OK.

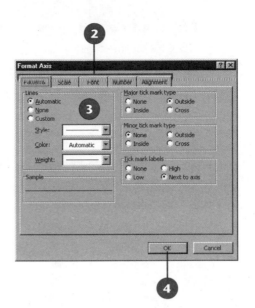

Customize a Chart

1. In Graph, select the chart.

2. Click the Chart menu, and then click Chart Options.

3. Click the tab (Titles, Axis, Gridlines, Legend, Data Labels, or Data Table) corresponding to the chart object you want to customize.

4. Make your changes.

5. Click OK.

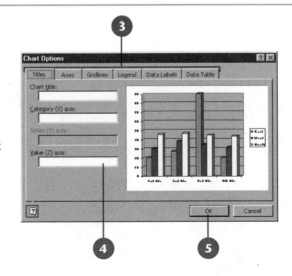

11

Creating an Organization Chart

An *organization chart* shows the personnel structure in a company or organization. You can create an organization chart, also known as an *org chart*, in any Office document with Microsoft Organization Chart. When you insert an org chart, *chart boxes* appear into which you enter the names and titles of company personnel. Each box is identified by its position in the chart. For example, Managers are at the top, Subordinates are below, Coworkers are to the sides, and so on.

TIP

Edit an org chart. *Double-click the organization chart, and then click the chart title or chart box you want to edit.*

TIP

Change an org chart style. *Click the Edit menu, point to Select, click All, click the Styles menu, and then click a chart style.*

Create a New Org Chart

1. Click the Insert menu, click Object, and then double-click MS Organization Chart 2.0.

2. Type a name in the open chart box.

3. Click a chart box type button on the toolbar, and then click the chart box to which you want to attach the new chart box.

4. Select the placeholder text, and then type a name or other text.

5. Click the File menu, and then click Exit And Return To Document1.

Enter your organization's name here.

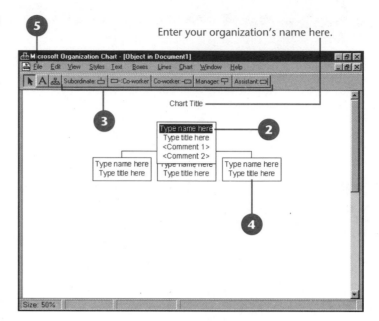

Open and Format an Org Chart

1. Double-click the org chart.

2. Click the Edit menu, point to Select, and select the items you want to format.

3. Click the Boxes or Lines menu, point to an item, and then click a format option.

4. Click the File menu, and then click Exit And Return To Document1.

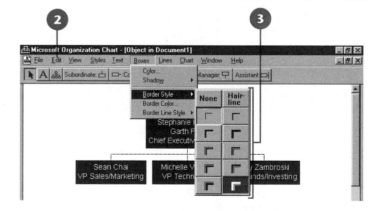

12

Creating a Web Site

World Wide Web technology is upgraded and perfected in Microsoft Publisher 2000. For better productivity and faster location of information, add *hyperlinks* (graphic objects or text you click to jump to other Office documents and intranet or Internet pages) to your publications. Do you want to create your own Web pages without spending any time learning the arcane HTML coding system used to format Web pages? The Web Page Wizard walks you through the process one step at a time. Publisher even provides several templates to start you off. In addition, you can save any publication as a Web page just as you would save a publication to your hard disk. Are you unsure how your publication's layout will look as a Web page? Preview it in Publisher or in your browser.

Professional Web Site Features

Web sites created in Publisher can have intriguing background colors and textures, as well as forms with option buttons, check boxes, list boxes, text boxes, and command buttons. You can also insert a navigation bar to ensure that readers have easy access to all the pages in your Web site.

Designing a Web Page

Web pages are multimedia documents that contain links. These links—also called hyperlinks, hypertext, or hypermedia—are highlighted text or graphics that you click to follow a pathway from one Web page to another. Linked Web pages, often called a *Web site*, are generally related by topic.

Web pages are based on *Hypertext Markup Language* (HTML)—a simple coding system used to format Web pages. A browser program, such as Microsoft Internet Explorer, interprets these special codes to determine how to display a Web page. Different codes mark the size, color, style, and placement of text and graphics. Codes also indicate which words and graphics are hyperlinks and to what files they link.

As the World Wide Web becomes a household term and many businesses create intranet and Internet Web sites—both of which use HTML documents—the ability to create, read, open, and save HTML documents directly from Publisher becomes an important time-saver.

HTML and Office 2000

All Office 2000 programs, including Publisher, use HTML as a companion file format. That means that Publisher, Word, Excel, PowerPoint, and Access, all can save and read HTML documents without any compatibility problems. And anyone with a browser can view your publications without worrying about whether their program, version, or computer system is different from yours.

Converting Publications to Web Pages

In addition to creating Web pages from scratch in Publisher, you can also save any existing document as a Web page to your hard disk drive, intranet, or Web server. These HTML publications preserve such features as styles, linked and embedded objects, and formatting attributes.

Each publication saved as an HTML document creates a handful of individual files. For example, each graphic in a publication becomes its own file. To make it easy to manage these multiple files, Publisher creates a folder with the same name, and in the same location, as the original HTML file for the publication. Any publication saved as a Web page consists of an HTML file and a folder that stores supporting files, such as a file for each graphic image.

Converting a Publication

You can easily convert a Publisher-designed newsletter or brochure to a Web site, and vice versa. When converting a publication, Publisher uses the original design—even if you've made changes to it on your own or with a wizard.

SEE ALSO

See "Adding a Hyperlink" on page 196 for information on inserting links on a Web page.

SEE ALSO

See "Applying Color to a Web Page" on page 199 to add colorful schemes and background textures to your Web pages.

Convert a Publication to a Web Site

1 If necessary, click the Show Wizard button.

2 Click Convert To Web Site.

3 Click Create.

4 Choose the option you want to use.

◆ Use the Web Site Wizard to automatically create a Web design with hyperlinks.

◆ Add your own hyperlinks and design your own layout.

5 Click OK.

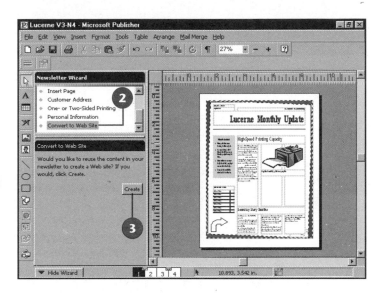

Convert a Web Site to a Publication

1 If necessary, click the Show Wizard button.

2 Click Convert To Print.

3 Click either the Newsletter or Brochure button.

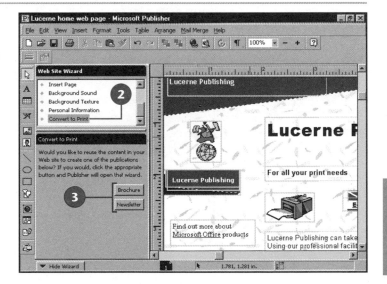

12

Creating a Web Page

The World Wide Web is your path to communicating with the greatest number of people without incurring printing and mailing costs. Use Publisher to create publications for your Web site. You can create Web pages that include text, calendars, schedules, special offers, price lists, and forms. You can use text and objects in your Web site to create hyperlinks to other Web pages. When you have completed your Web site, you can preview the Web pages as they will appear on the World Wide Web. Once you are satisfied with the Web site, you can use the Save As Web Page feature to save the publication for the Web.

TIP

Get Web site properties.
Open the Web site, click the File menu, click Web Properties, click the Site Or Page tab, make any changes, and then click OK.

Use the Web Sites Wizard

1. In the Catalog, click the Publications By Wizard tab.

2. Click Web Sites.

3. Click the thumbnail that displays the design you want for your Web site.

4. Click Start Wizard.

5. Click Next.

6. Choose a color scheme for your Web site, and then click Next.

   Publisher displays the first page (called the *home page*) of your Web site.

7. Click a check box for each page you want to include as part of your Web site, and then click Next. (Each option will appear on its own page.)

8. Indicate whether you want to include a form, and then click Next.

9. Indicate how you want the navigation bar to appear, and then click Next.

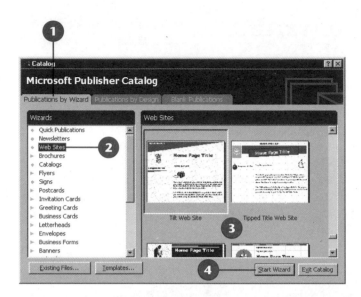

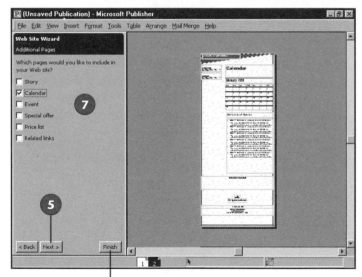

Click at any time to complete the wizard with default responses.

SEE ALSO

See "Previewing Web Pages" on page 208 for instructions on seeing how your Web pages will look on the Web.

SEE ALSO

See "Publishing to the Web" on page 210 for instructions on saving a publication in a Web file format.

SEE ALSO

See "Adding a Hyperlink" on page 196 for information on inserting hyperlinks in text and objects.

(10) Click Yes if you want a background sound to play when the home page opens, and then click Next.

(11) Click Yes if you want the background to appear textured, and then click Next.

(12) Choose the name and address information that you want to appear.

(13) Click Finish to create a Web site based on your responses to the wizard.

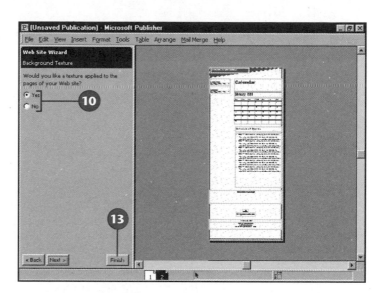

Create a Web Page from Scratch

(1) Click the File menu, and then click New.

(2) Click the Blank Publications tab, and then click Web Page.

(3) Click a Web page thumb-nail.

If you want, click the Custom Web Page button to adjust the Web page setup.

(4) Click Create.

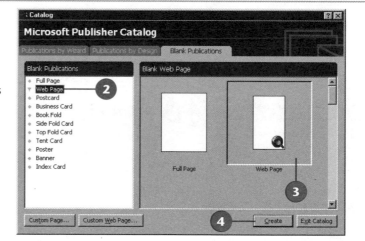

12

Adding a Hyperlink

When you reference information included earlier in a document, you traditionally had to duplicate material or add a footnote. Now you can create a *hyperlink*—a graphic object or colored, underlined text that you click to move (or *jump*) to a new location (or *destination*). The destination can be in the same document, another file on your computer or network, an e-mail address, or a Web page on your Intranet or the Internet.

Add a Hyperlink

1. Select the text you want to use as the hyperlink.

2. Click the Insert Hyperlink button on the Standard toolbar.

3. Click the option button for the location of your hyperlink.
   - Link to a Web site or Internet file.
   - Link to another page on your Web site.
   - Link to an Internet e-mail address.
   - Link to a file on your hard disk.

4. Type the address for the hyperlink, or click the Hyperlink Information drop-down arrow and select an entry from the list.

5. Click OK.

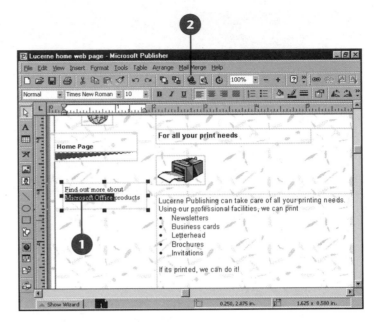

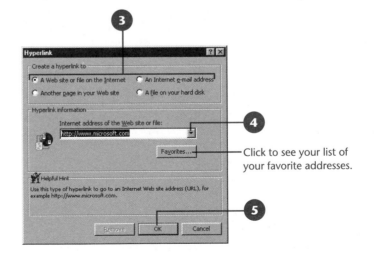

Click to see your list of your favorite addresses.

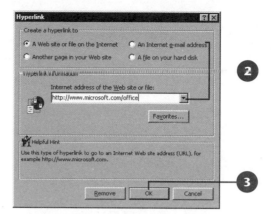

TIP

Format a hyperlink. *You can change the look of a hyperlink just as you do other text—select it and apply attributes. Drag the pointer over an existing hyperlink, and then use any Formatting toolbar buttons.*

TRY THIS

Replace hyperlink text.
Drag the I-beam pointer across an existing hyperlink to select it. Type the new text you want to use as the hyperlink to replace the selected text.

TIP

Delete a hyperlink. *You can always remove a hyperlink by deleting the object containing the link.*

SEE ALSO

See "Managing Web Page Graphics" on page 204 for information on adding a hyperlink to a graphic image.

Edit a Hyperlink

1. Right-click the hyperlink you want to edit, and then click Hyperlink.

2. Change the hyperlink type or the hyperlink information you want.

3. Click OK.

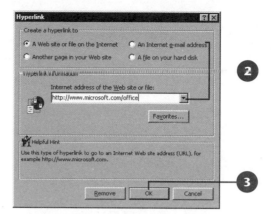

Remove a Hyperlink

1. Right-click the hyperlink you want to edit, and then click Hyperlink.

2. Click Remove.

3. Click OK.

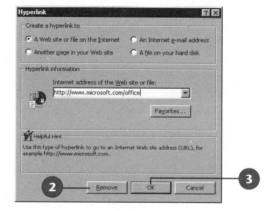

12

Creating a Hot Spot Hyperlink

You can specify a specific part of a publication or an object to be a hyperlink. This type of hyperlink is called a *hot spot*. An entire object can be a single hot spot or an object can contain multiple hot spots. Some objects, such as navigation buttons, contain a single hot spot that jumps you to a specific address. For other objects, such as a photo of a city, you can have several hot spots that link items in the photo to an address that provides information on the item.

Hot Spot Tool button

SEE ALSO

See "Managing Web Page Graphics" on page 204 for information on adding a hyperlink to a graphic image.

Create a Hot Spot Hyperlink

1 Open the Web page in which you want to add a hyperlink on a hot spot.

2 Click the Hot Spot Tool button on the Objects toolbar.

3 Drag to create a rectangle around the area you want a hot spot.

4 Click the hyperlink option button you want.

5 Enter the hyperlink Internet address.

6 Click OK.

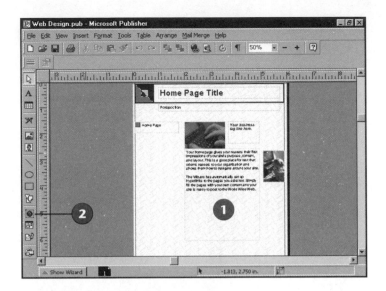

Applying Color to a Web Page

A basic Web page usually includes text, graphics, and hyperlinks. You can change the look of your Web site by selecting a color scheme—a predesigned layout containing a variety of colors for bullets, backgrounds, color, and lines to create specific moods. You can use the default color scheme or apply a custom one that you develop. Apply color schemes at any time—not just when you create the pages. You can also modify any color in a color scheme, and you can create and save your own custom color schemes.

Add Background Colors

1. Click the Format menu, and then click Color And Background Scheme.

2. Click the Standard tab.

3. Click an available scheme.

4. Click the Solid Color drop-down arrow, and then select a color.

5. If you want, click Browse to select a background, choose a background, and then click Open.

6. Click OK.

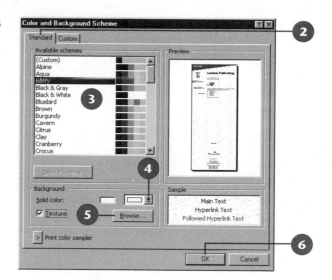

Create a Custom Scheme

1. Click the Format menu, and then click Color And Background Scheme.

2. Click the Custom tab.

3. Click any New drop-down arrow(s), and then select the colors you want.

4. Click Save Scheme, type a name for your scheme, and then click OK.

5. Click OK.

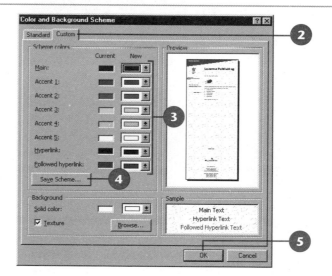

12

Creating a Form

In addition to providing information, you can also use your Web pages to collect data about current and potential visitors to your site. Using a variety of *form controls*—embedded objects that let visitors to your Web site indicate their responses to questions—you can collect demographic and preferential data that lets you know more about the people you serve. Form controls include single-line and multiline text boxes, check boxes, option buttons, and command buttons that let your visitors submit their responses.

TIP

Add a reply form using the Web Site Wizard. *If you know you want to have a reply form, add it when you're creating a Web site with the Web Site Wizard.*

Create a Reply Form

1. Click the Design Gallery Object button on the Objects toolbar.

2. Click the Objects by Category tab.

3. Click the Web Reply Forms category.

4. Click a Web Reply Forms sample.

5. Click Insert Object.

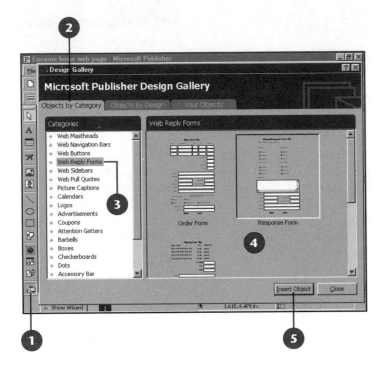

Make responding easy. *Any questions on your Web site should be simple and straight-forward. Avoid ambiguous, time-consuming, or lengthy questions. Questions that are difficult for respondents to answer will probably not give you the relevant, honest data you want.*

Add Form Controls

1. Click the Form Control button on the Objects toolbar.

2. Click the Form Control you want to add.

   ◆ Use a single-line text box to provide one line for user input.

   ◆ Use a multiline text box to provide many lines for user input.

   ◆ Use a check box to offer a Yes or No choice.

   ◆ Use a group of option buttons to offer multiple choices.

   ◆ Use a list box to present a group of items in a list.

   ◆ Use a command button (such as Submit or Reset) to allow visitors to send their responses.

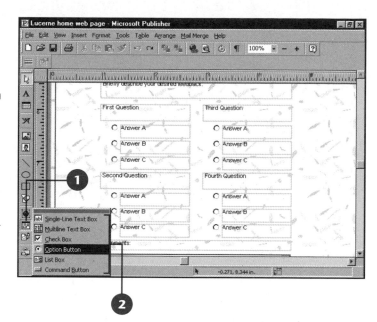

12

Modifying a Form Control

Have you ever completed a form and noticed that some check boxes and option buttons were already selected? You can easily modify your Web page form controls to make form completion easier for your respondents. You can set form control properties so that a specific response for an option button, check box, or list item is the default. This makes it faster for users to complete the form.

You can also align form controls to make their appearance more pleasing and professional.

Change Form Control Properties

1 Right-click the form control.

2 Click Option Button Properties on the shortcut menu.

Your form control properties menu item will vary according to the form control you've created.

3 Click an Appearance option button.

◆ Choose Selected for the control to be the default selection.

◆ Choose Not Selected for the control to not be the default selection.

4 Click the Return Data With This Label drop-down arrow, and then select a name that will be identified as the question group.

5 Type an Option Button Value (or label) for the specific control.

6 Click OK.

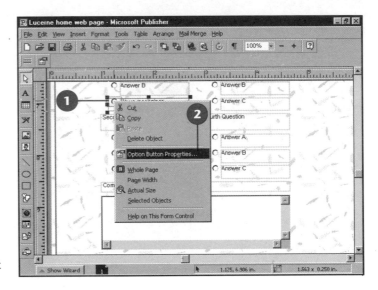

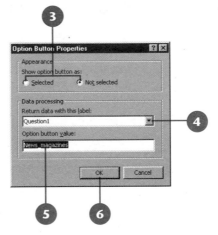

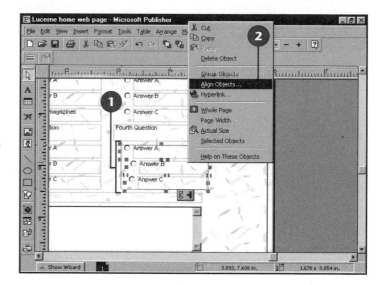

TIP

Align objects last. *Once you confirm the type and content of form controls, concentrate on position. That way, you'll have to make fewer alignment changes later.*

TRY THIS

Experiment with alignment. *Try using several types of alignment on form controls until you find one that looks best.*

SEE ALSO

See "Aligning Objects" on page 110 for information on different ways of lining up objects.

Align Form Controls

1. Press and hold Shift as you click each control you want to align.

2. Right-click the controls, and then click Align Objects.

3. Click any alignment option in the Left To Right or Top To Bottom areas of the dialog box.

4. Click OK.

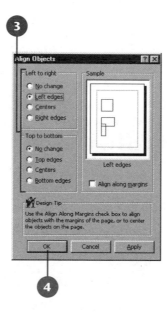

Managing Web Page Graphics

As in any publication, graphic images provide visual relief and add a professional dimension to your Web site.

Design Gallery elements, particularly those matching your current theme, can easily be added to your Web page. Any graphic image—even one from the Design Gallery—can become an integral part of your Web site if you add a hyperlink to it. For example, your Web page could include a hyperlink image that a user could click to send you an e-mail message.

TIP

Consider screen resolution and image size. *To be truly effective, a user should not have to scroll to see an entire image. Make sure this is the case by previewing your Web pages using a resolution of 640 x 480.*

Add Design Gallery Elements

1. Click the Design Gallery Object button on the Object toolbar.

2. Click a category.

3. Click a thumbnail from the category.

4. Click Insert Object.

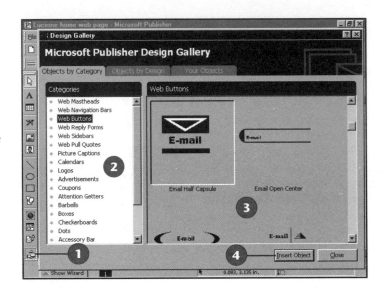

Add a Hyperlink to a Graphic Image

1. Right-click the image, and then click Hyperlink.

2. Click the type of hyperlink you want to create.

3. Click the Hyperlink Information drop-down arrow and supply any necessary information.

4. Click OK.

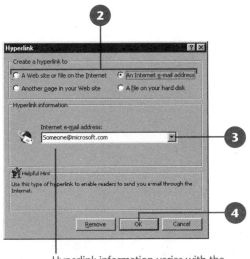

Hyperlink information varies with the type of hyperlink being created.

TIP

Clip Gallery Tool button. *If you use this Objects toolbar button, you have to draw a frame for the artwork before the Clip Gallery opens.*

SEE ALSO

See "Adding a Hyperlink" on page 196 for instructions on creating text hyperlinks.

SEE ALSO

See "Inserting a Picture" on page 86 for information on finding and inserting clip art from the Clip Gallery.

SEE ALSO

See "Cropping a Graphic Image" on page 89 for instructions on modifying visible areas of a graphic image.

Add an Animated Picture from the Clip Gallery

① Click the Insert menu, point to Picture, and then click Clip Art.

② Click the Motion Clips tab.

③ Click a Category.

④ Click an image, and then click the Insert Clip button.

⑤ Click the close button on the Insert ClipArt dialog box.

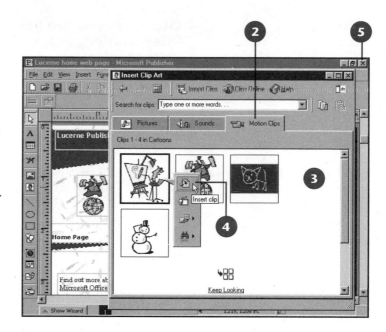

12

Using a Navigation Bar

A navigation bar is an important part of any well-designed multipage Web site. A *navigation bar* is either vertical or horizontal in design, and contains hyperlinks to other pages within your Web site. With this feature, your readers will be able to jump quickly and easily to your other pages. The Design Gallery contains a variety of predesigned navigation bars that you can easily insert in your Web page. Many of the Design Gallery elements are smart objects, so any change to coloring or formatting of a navigation bar will result in automatic updates elsewhere.

SEE ALSO

See "Adding a Hyperlink" on page 196 for information on creating links.

Create a Navigation Bar Using the Design Gallery

1. Click the Design Gallery Object button on the Objects toolbar.

2. Click the Objects By Category or Objects By Design tab.

3. Click the Web Navigation Bars category.

4. Click a navigation bar thumbnail.

5. Click Insert Object.

6. If you want, drag the object to a new location.

7. If necessary, click the Wizard button to change the navigation button style.

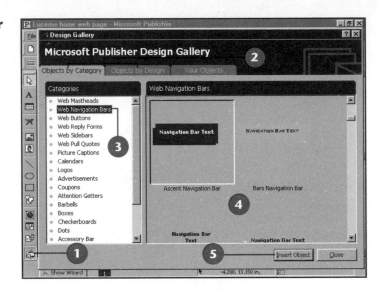

Change the design of the navigation bar to any of these styles.

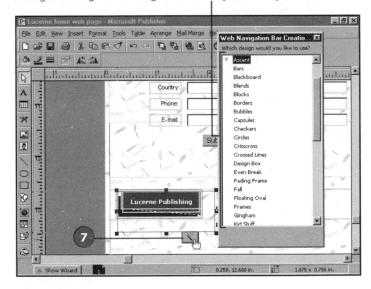

Adding HTML Codes

Publisher's Web Site Wizard does a great job of creating a Web site for you. Still, you may find you want to add additional code to your pages. You can add HTML code fragments—your own codes—that create effects such as a counter or a scrolling marquee. Your code fragments can consist of HTML code, ActiveX, VBScript, or Java applets.

You can edit and view code fragments in your browser, just like the pages prepared by the wizard.

SEE ALSO

See "Previewing Web Pages" on page 208 for information on seeing your Web pages in a browser.

Add an HTML Code Fragment

1. Click the Insert menu, and then click HTML Code Fragment.

2. Drag the pointer to create a frame where you want the code fragment to appear.

3. Type the code fragment.

4. Click OK.

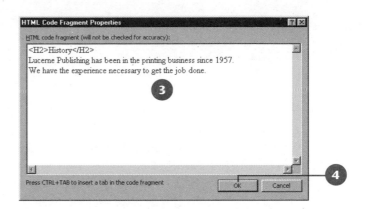

Edit an HTML Code Fragment

1. Double-click the HTML code fragment.

2. Modify the text in the HTML Code Fragment Properties dialog box.

3. Click OK.

Additional text added

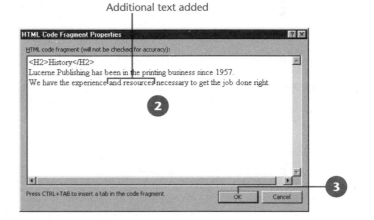

12

Previewing Web Pages

After you create a Web page, you should preview it in a Web browser, such as Microsoft Internet Explorer, to confirm the placement of stories, graphics, and other objects. *Web Page Preview* displays the open file in your default browser even if you haven't saved it yet.

TIP

Change your screen resolution. *640 x 480 is the lowest screen resolution a reader will probably use. Use this setting to view your Web pages.*

TIP

High-fidelity display. *Publisher takes advantage of HTML 4.0 and Cascading Style Sheet technology.*

TIP

Different browsers give different results. *Not everyone uses the same type of browser. Your Web page might look different on a different type of browser.*

Preview a Web Page in a Browser

1 Open the Web page you want to preview.

2 Click the Web Page Preview button on the Standard toolbar.

Your default Web browser starts and displays the Web page.

3 Scroll to view the entire page, click hyperlinks to test them, and so forth.

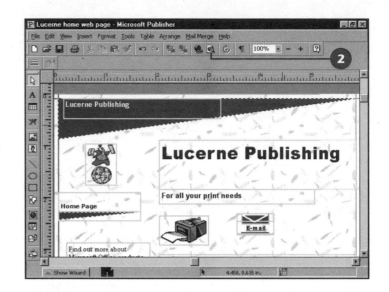

Animated artwork displays just as it would on the Web.

Saving a Web Page

You can save any publication as a Web page. You can then use a browser to view and even edit your publication over the Internet or an intranet. You can continue to open and work with the publication from Publisher without having to convert to the original format. Web pages use *Hypertext Markup Language* (HTML)—a simple coding system that specifies the formats a browser uses to display the document.

Any publication saved as a Web page consists of an HTML file and a folder that stores supporting files, such as a file for each graphic. Publisher automatically selects the appropriate format for your graphics based on the their origin.

SEE ALSO

See "Adding HTML Codes" on page 207 for information about manually adding HTML code fragments.

Save a Publication as a Web Page

1. Open the publication you want to save as a Web page.

2. Click the File menu, and then click Create Web Site From Current Publication.

3. Click the Use The Web Site Wizard To Automatically Create A Web Design With Hyperlinks option button, or the Add My Own Hyperlinks And Do My Own Web Layout option button.

4. Click OK.

5. Click Yes to save changes and then convert the publication to a Web format, or click No to convert the publication without saving additional changes.

6. Make any additional changes using the Web Site Wizard.

7. Click the File menu, and then click Save As Web Page.

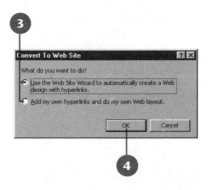

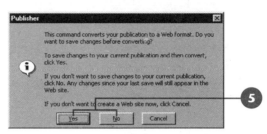

12

Publishing to the Web

Once your Web pages are complete, you'll want to publish a copy of your publication in HTML format directly to a *Web server* (a computer on the Internet or intranet that stores Web pages) so others can view and manipulate your data. Publishing to a Web server is as simple as saving a file. With the Microsoft Web Publishing Wizard, you can easily post your files on the Internet for others to view.

TIP

Special installation. *Make sure the Microsoft Web Publishing Wizard has been installed on your computer.*

SEE ALSO

See "Saving a Web Page" on page 209 for instructions on saving a publication in HTML format.

Publish to the Web Using the Microsoft Web Publishing Wizard

1. Click the Start button on the Windows taskbar, point to Programs, point to Accessories, point to Internet Tools, and then click Web Publishing Wizard.

2. Click Next to continue.

3. Click the File Or Folder Name drop-down arrow and select a file, or click the Browse Folders or Browse Files button and locate the file you want to publish.

4. Click Next to continue.

You may need to install this wizard from the Publisher 2000 CD-ROM.

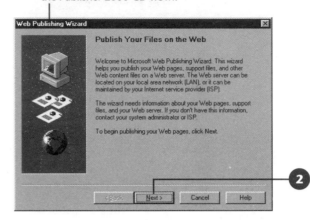

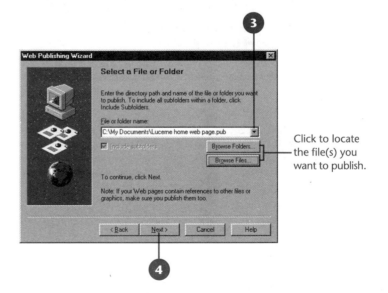

Click to locate the file(s) you want to publish.

TIP

Manage your Web files. *You can add, move, or delete files stored on a Web server from the Windows Explorer just as you would with a file server.*

SEE ALSO

See "Previewing Web Pages" on page 208 to preview your publication in a Web browser.

TIP

Preview files in a browser. *Before publishing to the Web, make sure you've previewed the files in your browser. Look for misspellings, inconsistencies, or anything that just doesn't look right.*

(5) Type a name in the Descriptive Name box, and then click Next to continue.

(6) Establish an Internet connection, type the Internet address where you want your site to be published in the URL Or Internet Address box, verify the correct local address in the Local Directory box, and then click Next to continue.

(7) Click Next to continue.

(8) Supply the FTP server name where your files will be published.

(9) Click Next to continue.

(10) Click Finish.

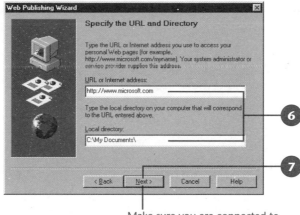

Make sure you are connected to the Internet before proceeding.

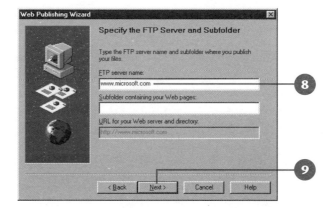

12

Using Mail Merge

Grab attention with personalized publications. Whether it's a flyer, invitation, brochure, or newsletter, you can add personal information anywhere within the publication to each copy that you print. You can even insert mailing addresses on newsletters, envelopes, or labels.

Personalize Your Publications

The most common use for mail merge is to create mailing labels, envelopes, or address blocks on publications. You create a publication and prepare the printed copies for mailing in Microsoft Publisher 2000. The only thing Publisher doesn't do is lick the stamps.

The merge process also lets you individually customize any publication. Impress clients, business associates, social groups, or even family members by adding personal information to their copy. List birthdays in the team's newsletter. Invite family and friends by name to a party.

Just create a formatted publication with the text, tables, pictures, and anything else that won't change. Any data that changes from person to person goes into another file, which you combine with the publication. In a snap, you've got personalized publications.

Mail Merge Fundamentals

Did you ever send the same flyer, brochure, or newsletter to several people and spend a lot of time entering personal information, such as names and addresses? If so, mail merge will save you time.

Mail merge is the process of combining names and addresses (or other individual information) stored in a data source with standard, unchanging text in a main publication to produce customized documents. Let's look at each part of the process in turn.

There are three main steps to merging. First, create a data source with the variable information. Second, create the main document with the unchanging information and placeholders for the variable information. Finally, merge the two.

Create the Data Source

A *data source* is the document that contains the variable information you want to insert in a publication. This can include names, street addresses, titles, favorite colors, or any other information that changes from person to person. In Publisher, the data source is called an *address list*, although you can include other types of information as well.

You enter each type of information into a separate category, called a *field*. For example, you might include the fields First Name, Last Name, and City in an address list. The specific information you enter for each person for the entire collection of fields is called an *entry*.

Create the Main Publication

A *main publication* is any publication to which you insert the variable information from an address list. You can turn any existing publication into a main publication or you can create a new publication to use. Make sure the main publication includes all the text, tables, pictures, art, and so forth that you want to appear in every copy. Format the layout and elements just as you would a regular publication.

Then insert the *field codes*, placeholder text that shows Publisher where to insert the particular item of information from the address list into your publication.

For example, you could include a headline on a newsletter, such as: "Ketan Dalal, you'll love our sale prices!" The main document would include the field codes for the name followed by the standard text: "<<First Name>> <<Last Name>>, you'll love our sales prices!"

Perform the Merge

The final step in the process is to *merge*, or combine, the main document that includes the field codes with the address list that contains the individual information. Publisher creates a new document for each entry in the address list. For example, if your address list includes entries for 45 customers, then Publisher creates 45 newsletters, each with a personal headline.

Creating a Main Publication

You can use any publication in a mail merge. The *main publication* is a publication, whether you created it from a template or from scratch, that contains the standard text you want to print and *field codes,* or placeholders, for the variable information. Standard text is anything—text, tables, pictures—you want to print on every copy. Variable information is the specific text you want to change for each copy.

Create Labels or Envelopes

1. Click the New button on the Standard toolbar to create a new, blank publication, if necessary.

2. Click the File menu, and then click Page Setup.

3. Click the Labels or Envelopes option button.

4. Select the label brand and style or the envelope size.

5. Click OK.

A label or envelope appears in the publication.

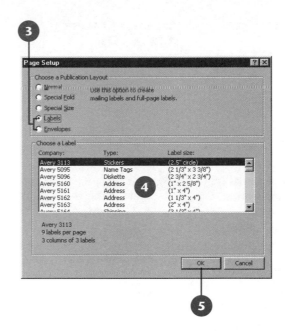

Creating a Data Source

A data source is a file in which you store variable information, such as names, addresses, prices, birthdays, and so on. Each specific type of information is stored in a field. The specific information you enter in each field for one person is called an entry. In Publisher, the data source is called an address list (although you can include other types of information as well). The easiest way to create an address list is to open a new address list and then add, delete, or rename the fields to fit your purpose. Then enter the specific information for each person.

TIP

Reorder the field list. *Click the name of the field you want to move, and then click the Move Up and Move Down buttons in the Customize Address List dialog box.*

Create a Custom Address List

1 Click the Mail Merge menu, and then click Create Publisher Address List.

2 Click Customize in the New Address List dialog box.

3 Select the field above or below which you want to add the new field.

4 Click Add.

5 Type a name for the new field.

6 Select where to add the field.

7 Click OK.

8 Repeat steps 3 through 7 for each field you want to add.

9 To delete a field name, select the field, click Delete, and then click the Yes button.

10 To rename a field, select the field, click Rename, type a new name, and then click OK.

11 When you're done, click OK.

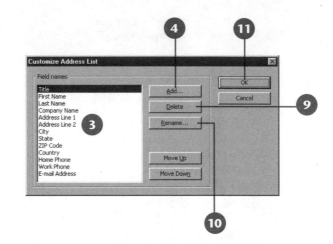

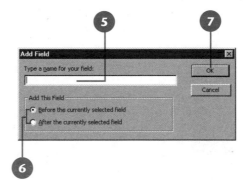

Enter Information in an Address List

1. Click the Mail Merge menu, and then click Create Publisher Address List.

2. Type the information for the first field.

   Type only those spaces or punctuation you want to always print with the field.

3. Press Tab to move to the next field.

   When you press Tab in the last field, a new entry opens.

4. Repeat steps 2 and 3 for each field in each entry.

5. When you're done, click Close.

   The Save As dialog box appears.

6. Type a name for the address list.

7. Click the Save In drop-down arrow, and then select a location to store the address list.

8. Click Save.

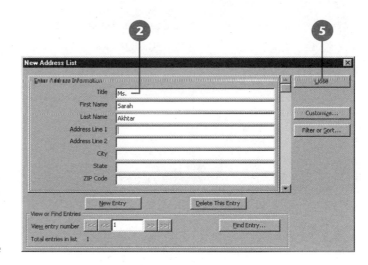

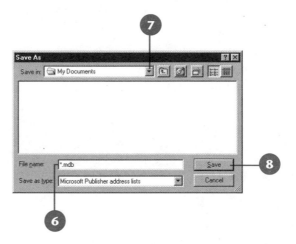

Editing a Publisher Address List

A Publisher address list has the flexibility to grow and change with your needs. You can use the same address list with multiple publications. Over time, you may find that you want to add new entries, update, or correct information in an existing entry, or delete entries that are no longer appropriate. You can modify an existing address list. Just open the address list you want to edit. Then you can edit existing entries, delete unnecessary entries, or use the Find feature to locate a specific entry quickly.

Open an Address List

1. Click the Mail Merge menu, and then click Edit Publisher Address List.

2. Click the Look In drop-down arrow, and then select the drive and folder with the address list you want to edit.

3. Double-click the address list you want to edit.

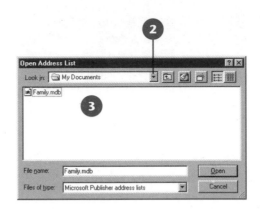

Modify Address List Information

1. Open the address list you want to modify.

2. Find the entry you want to edit.

3. Click in the field and make your edits.

   Publisher saves your edits as you work.

4. Repeat steps 2 and 3 for each field you want to edit.

5. When you're done, click Close.

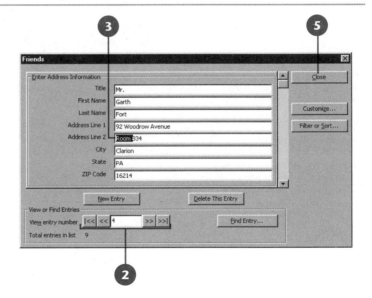

TIP

Add a new entry. *Add a new entry to the address list the way you did when creating the list. Click the Add New Entry button or press Tab in the last record. Then enter the information in each field as usual.*

TIP

Modify the fields in an address list. *You add, rename, and delete field names in an existing address list the same way as you add, rename, or edit a new one.*

SEE ALSO

See "Creating a Data Source" on page 216 for more information about adding, renaming, and deleting field names in an address list.

TRY THIS

Find specific entries. *Open an address list, and use the view buttons to move from entry to entry. Click Find Entry to locate all entries from your state. Then locate all entries whose last name starts with the letter s. Finally, locate the last record in the address list.*

TIP

Deleted entries are unrecoverable. *You cannot undo the deletion of an entry in an address list. Once the entry is deleted, the information is lost.*

Find an Entry

1. Open the address list in which you want to find an entry.

2. Click Find Entry.

3. Enter the text you want to find.

4. If you want to search a specific field, click the This Field option button, and then click the This Field drop-down arrow and select the field name.

5. Click Find Next.

6. Click Close, and then click Close in the address list.

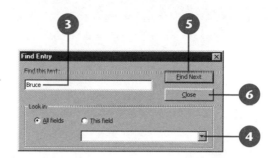

Delete an Entry

1. Open the address list from which you want to delete an entry.

2. View the entry you want to delete.

3. Click Delete This Entry.

4. Click Yes to confirm the deletion.

5. Click Close.

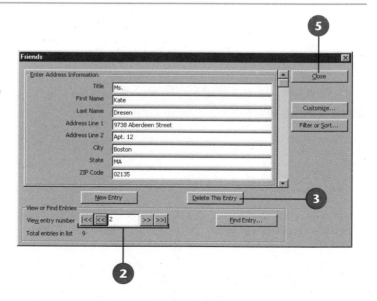

Connecting to a Data Source

After you set up your main publication, you need to connect it to a data source. But what if the information you want to merge with your publication already exists in another program? Although it is best to use a Publisher address list as the data source, you can use other types of files as well. For example, if you store all your contact information in Outlook, try connecting the contact list to your publication as the data source. Other types of files you can use as a data source include a table in a Word document or a database such as Access.

Use an Existing Data Source

1. Create or click in the text frame or table cell that contains the variable information.

2. Click the Mail Merge menu, and then click Open Data Source.

3. Click Merge Information From Another Type Of File.

4. Double-click the filename.

5. Insert fields as usual, and then click Close.

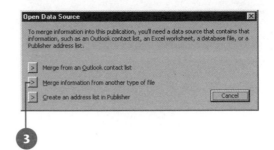

Use an Outlook Contact List

1. Create a text frame for the variable information, click the Mail Merge menu, and then click Open Data Source.

2. Click Merge From An Outlook Contact List.

3. Click a profile in the Profile Name list (if Outlook isn't running), and then click OK.

4. Click a contact list in the Choose Contact List dialog box, and then click OK.

5. Insert fields as usual, and then click Close.

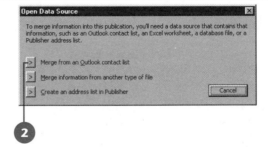

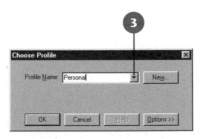

Inserting Field Codes

After you connect your main publication to a data source, you add the field codes. *Field codes* are placeholders telling Publisher where to get the variable information you specify. You insert field codes into a text frame or a table cell. The Insert Field dialog box stays open so you can add spaces or punctuation between the field codes, move the insertion point, or create a new frame. You can insert multiple field codes into one text frame or cell.

TIP

Format field codes. *To get the exact formatting you want for merged variable information, format the field codes just like regular text.*

TIP

Copy or move field codes. *Select the field code, and then use the Cut, Copy, or Paste features, or drag-and-drop it as usual.*

Insert Field Codes

1 Create a text frame or table cell or click in an existing one where you want the variable information to appear.

2 Click the Mail Merge menu, and then click Insert Field.

3 Double-click the name of the first field you want to insert.

4 Type any necessary spaces, punctuation, or returns to set up your fields correctly.

For example:
<<City>>, <<State>>
Dear <<First Name>>:

5 Repeat steps 1 through 3 for each field code you want to insert.

6 When you're done, click Close.

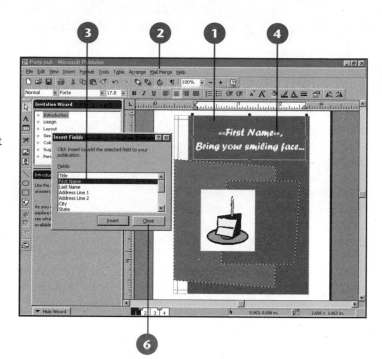

Merging a List into a Publication

After you finish inserting field codes, you can merge the publication with an address list. This displays the publication with the information from the first entry of your address list. Viewing the merge results is a good way to verify that the address list is correct, field codes are placed correctly, appropriate spaces appear around the codes, and all the punctuation is correct. If you connected the publication to the wrong address list, you can change the data source. As long as the field names in the new data source are the same, the publication will display the new entries. Otherwise, you need to replace the old field codes with new ones.

TIP

Connect to a data source.
Before you can merge a publication, it must be connected to a data source.

Merge a Publication and Data Source

1. Create the main publication.

2. Create the data source.

3. Insert field codes.

4. Click the Mail Merge menu, and then click Merge.

5. Click Close.

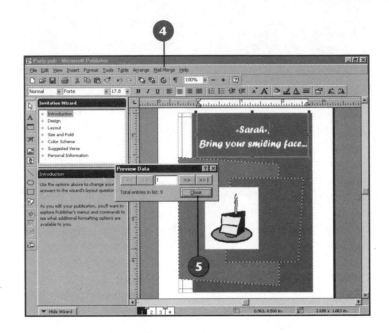

View Merge Results

1. Click the Mail Merge menu, and then click Show Merge Results.

2. Click the Next button to move ahead one entry.

3. Click the Previous button to move back one entry.

4. Click the Home button to move to the first entry.

5. Click the End button to move to the last entry.

6. Type a number to jump to that entry.

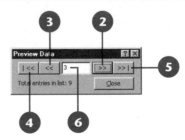

Change the Data Source

1. Open the merged publication.

2. Click the Mail Merge menu, and then click Open Data Source.

3. Click the Yes button to confirm you want to change the data source.

4. Click Merge Information From A File I Already Have.

5. Click the Look In drop-down arrow, and then select the location of the new data source, and then double-click its filename.

6. If necessary, click OK.

7. Insert field codes from the new data source, as needed.

8. Delete "<<missing mail merge field>>" placeholders, as needed.

9. Click Close.

10. Click the Mail Merge menu, and then click Merge.

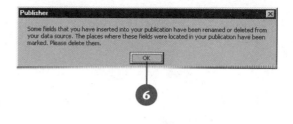

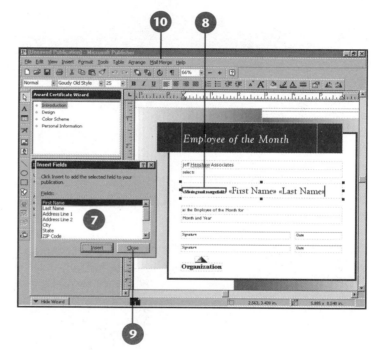

Filtering or Sorting a Merged Publication

Do you want to merge only certain entries from your address list? Then *filter* the list to show only those entries that meet specific criteria, such as State equal to California. You can create up to three filter criteria for a data source and choose whether the entry must meet one, two, or all three criteria to be included. A filter doesn't delete entries from data source, it just hides them from view. *Sorting* changes the order of address list entries in a merged publication. You can sort by up to three levels, such as by zip code for mailing labels, or by last name and then first for name tabs.

TIP

And or Or? *To filter using And, entries must meet all criteria included; to filter using Or, entries must meet criteria for either filter included.*

Filter an Address List

1. Open a merged publication, click the Mail Merge menu, and then click Filter Or Sort.

2. Click the Filter tab.

3. Click the Field drop-down arrow, and select a field name.

4. Click the Comparison drop-down arrow, and select a phrase.

5. Type the text or numbers to which you want to compare the selected field.

6. Click OK.

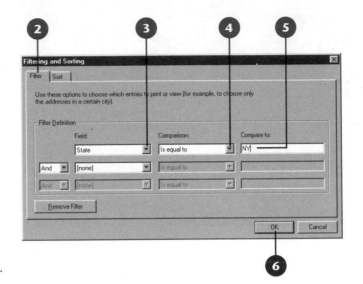

Specify Multiple Criteria

1. In the Filtering And Sorting dialog box, set up the first filter for the merged publication as usual.

2. Select And or Or from the list box in the second row (the second filter).

3. Set up the second filter.

4. Repeat steps 2 and 3 for the third filter (third row), if necessary.

5. Click OK.

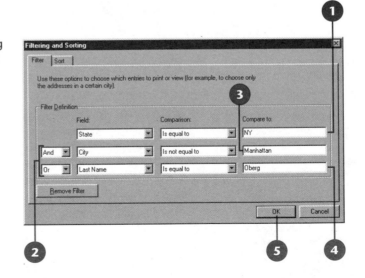

Remove a filter or sort.
Open a filtered or sorted merged publication, click the Mail Merge menu, click Filter Or Sort, click Remove Filter on the Filter tab or Remove Sort on the Sort tab, and then click OK.

Sort or filter an address list directly. *You can filter or sort the address list (rather than the merged publication). Click the Mail Merge menu, click Edit Publisher Address List, open the address list, and then click Filter Or Sort. Follow the same steps to filter or sort a merged document. Only the address list is affected; the merged publication will not print or preview this way.*

Sort and filter a merged publication. *Open the merged publication, filter the list for all entries from New York state, and then sort the filtered entries to print in ascending order by last name.*

Ascending or descending order. *Ascending orders entries A to Z, 1-9, or earliest to latest. Descending orders them in just the opposite way.*

Sort an Address List

1 Open the merged publication you want to sort, click the Mail Merge menu, and then click Filter Or Sort.

2 Click the Sort tab.

3 Click the Sort By This Field drop-down arrow, and then select the field name you want to sort by.

4 Select the sort order.

5 Click the Then By This Field drop-down arrow, and then select the field name you want to sort by.

6 Select the sort order.

7 Click the second Then Sort By This Field drop-down arrow, and then select the field name you want to sort by.

8 Select the sort order.

9 Click OK.

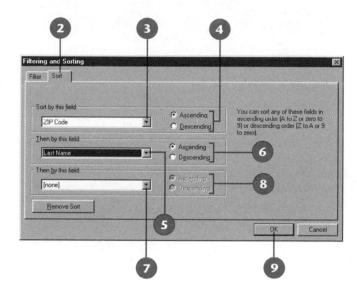

Creating Merged Labels

Using mail merge to create mailing labels turns a potentially tedious job into a relatively easy one. You can purchase blank, adhesive mailing labels for a laser printer. Publisher includes templates for Avery labels and even some specially designed labels from PaperDirect. Whatever brand or size of label you use, the process for creating them is the same. First you create a label publication. Then you open the data source with the address information you want to use and insert merge fields into the label publication. Finally you merge the document, verify the labels, and print.

Create a Label Main Publication

1 Click the File menu, and then click New.

2 Click Labels.

3 Double-click the label thumbnail.

4 Answer the Label Wizard questions, clicking Next and Finish as appropriate.

5 Click the Save button on the Standard toolbar to save to a file.

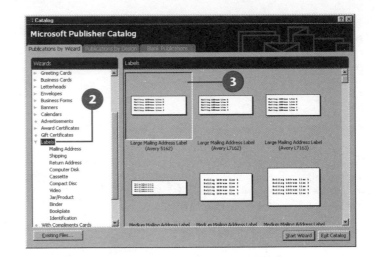

Insert Merge Fields

1 Click the recipient address field box to select it.

2 Click the Mail Merge menu, and then click Open Data Source.

3 Select the source document and open it.

4 Double-click a field name in the Insert Fields dialog box.

5 Insert the appropriate fields, spacing, and punctuation.

6 When you're done, click Close.

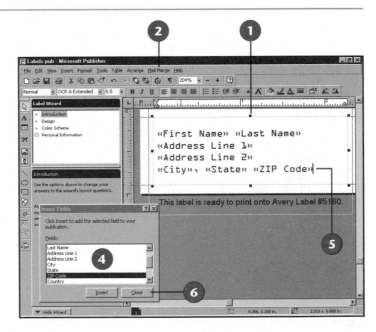

Postal Service preferred addressing format. *The postal service prefers mailing labels that are addressed and formatted in a way that improves the accuracy of their automated readers. The delivery addresses should be in all uppercase letters or in a sans serif font, such as Arial. The delivery address should include in order:*
(1) optional non-address data;
(2) any information or attention line;
(3) recipient's name;
(4) street address complete with apartment or suite numbers and delivery designations, such as RD, ST, or NW;
(5) city, state, and postal code (ZIP+4);
(6) country name, if needed, in all uppercase letters.
Omit all punctuation except the hyphen in the ZIP+4 code.

Create mailing labels for your next party. *Rather than hand-addressing the envelopes for your next party invitations, try using merged mailing labels to address them. And while you're at it, why not personalize the invitations as well?*

Merge Data Source and Labels

1. Click the Mail Merge menu, and then click Merge.

2. Preview the merged labels with data to verify the spacing and variable information.

3. Click Close.

4. Make any changes as needed to the merged label.

5. Format the fields as needed.

6. Filter or sort the merged publication as needed.

7. Click the Mail Merge menu, and then click Show Merge Results to view the data.

8. When you're done, click Close.

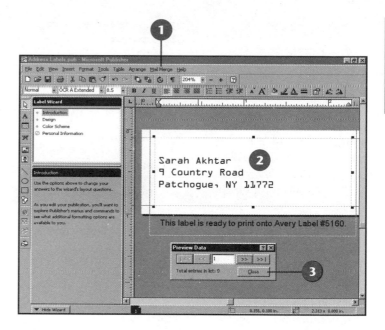

Printing a Merged Publication

The final step in producing a merged publication is to print it. To print the merged publication quickly, you can use the Print button on the Standard toolbar. To choose options, you need to open the Print dialog box. By default, Publisher closes up any extra lines or spaces left by fields in your address list that don't contain any information. You can also select whether to print publications for all entries or for a selected range of entries. It is also a good idea to print a test before printing all the merged publications on the final paper. A test prints a publication for the first entry or the first two rows of labels.

Print a Merged Document

1. Open the merged publication.

2. Click the File menu, and then click Print Merge.

3. If you want blank lines to print for empty fields in your address list, click to clear the Don't Print Lines That Contain Only Empty Fields check box.

4. Select all entries or a range of entries to print.

5. Click OK.

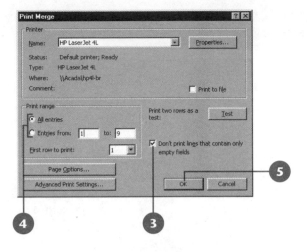

Print a Test

1. Open the merged publication.

2. Click the File menu, and then click Print Merge.

3. Click Test.

4. Click OK to print the entire publication or click Cancel to close the dialog box.

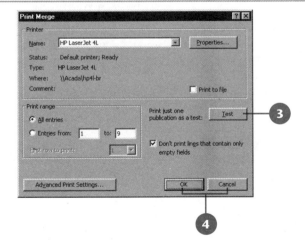

14

Printing Your Publication

The final step in creating your publication is printing it. Depending on the number of copies you need and the color and print quality you want, there are several ways you can output your finished publication. You can print on your trusty desktop printer (whether black-and-white or color, laser or inkjet). Or, if you need more copies or higher quality, visit your local copy shop or contact a commercial printer.

Working with a Commercial Printing Service

There are two main types of commercial printing services, traditional and digital. Traditional printers generate either film or press plates from your files. Digital printers generate multiple copies of your publication directly from your files.

Depending on your design and your budget, Publisher can generate full color, spot-color, and black and white documents for a commercial printing service. Full color output is the most expensive option. Spot color is a good alternative, because it allows you to add one or two accent colors to a design at a relatively low cost. Black and white is the least expensive option, because it restricts your color choices to black, white, and shades of gray.

Types of Printers

Desktop Printing

A desktop printer's main advantage is convenience. It's ready to print whenever you are. You no longer have to sacrifice quality for this convenience. Depending on your printer and paper, you can get medium to very good quality for a fairly low cost. In addition, desktop printing has burst into color in the last few years. Use desktop printing for a limited number of final copies; personalized mailings using Publisher's mail merge features; master copies to duplicate at a copy shop; labels, envelopes, and other odd-sized or hand-fed items; special papers for business cards, letterhead, and so forth; or interim copies for proofing.

Copy Shop Printing

If you need more copies or better quality than your desktop printer provides, try a copy shop. Within 24 hours, you can get 500 or more medium quality copies. Also, the copy shop can print double-sided (both the front and back of a sheet), *fold* sheets into booklets, *trim* away the ragged edge, or *bind* sheets with a plastic spiral. You choose the paper you want from the shop's collection (including color, texture, weight, and sizes up to 11 x 17 inches). Desktop printers often can't print on heavier or larger sizes of paper. Use copy shop printing for better quality or higher quantity than a desktop printer pro-vides, double-sided copies, paper sizes up to 11 x 17 inches, fewer than 500 copies, publications with camera-ready photos or graphics, or quick turnaround (usually 24 hours).

Commercial Printing

If you need higher quality output, or if you're printing a large quantity or using process and spot inks, try a commercial printing service. *Commercial printing* typically refers to printing on high-capacity, high-resolution presses.

Before printing, a pre-press check verifies all graphic files and fonts are available and in the right format, and print settings are correct. Then, an *Imagesetter* (a high-resolution imaging device) creates color separations of your publication on film or photographic paper. The press plates for printing are created from this film. Before printing, you receive a proof (called a *blueline*) to check page sequence and element placement. If necessary, use a color proof to verify color matching and registration.

Use commercial printing for high-quality, long-lasting, and smudge-free output; at least 500 copies; high-resolution reproduction of color photos or graphics; spot color, such as a specific colored logo; or unusual or large paper sizes (up to 26 x 36 inches).

Printing on a Desktop Printer

For most of the publications you print, you'll want to use the same printer. You can set this printer as your default—the printer that appears in the Print Setup and Print dialog boxes. For example, you might want to set a black-and-white laser printer as your default printer and then switch to a color inkjet printer only when you're ready to print your final publication.

> **TIP**
>
> **Missing printer?** *You may need to add the printer driver. This is often necessary when you plan to print a publication at a printing service and need to set up your publication for their printer.*

> **TIP**
>
> **Add a desktop printer to the printer list.** *Click Start, point to Settings, click Printers, and double-click the Add Printer icon. Answer the Printer Wizard's questions, clicking Next after each one. Click Finish when you're done.*

Choose a Default Printer

1. Click the Start button on the taskbar, point to Settings, and then click Printers.

2. Click the printer you want to use as the default.

3. Click the File menu, and then click Set As Default.

   Any publications you open adjust to the new default printer's settings.

4. Click the Close button.

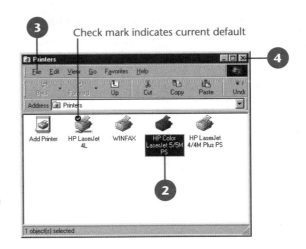

Check mark indicates current default

Choose a Different Printer

1. Click the File menu, and then click Print Setup or Print.

2. Click the Name drop-down arrow, and then select the printer you want to use.

3. Click OK.

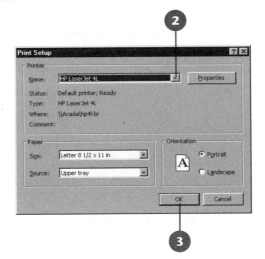

14

Printing on a Color Desktop Printer

The colors you see on the screen depend on your monitor and system settings; the colors you see in a printed publication depend on your printer. You can use the color sampler publication to compare color differences between your screen and printed publication. Then you can have Publisher mark which colors won't print well so you can adjust them.

> **TIP**
>
> **Adjust colors.** *Click an object, click the Format menu, point to Fill Color, and then click More Colors. Click to select the Mark Colors That Will Not Print Well On My Printer check box. Click OK. Colors that don't print well have an X in the color palette.*

Print a Color Sampler

1. Click the Format menu, and then click Color Scheme.

2. Click the Standard tab.

3. Click Print Color Sampler.

4. Click OK.

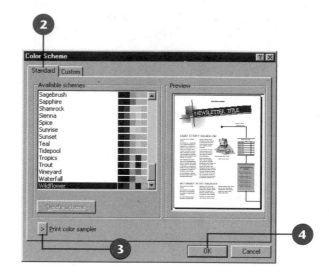

Mark Colors That Won't Print Well

1. Choose your color printer.

2. Click the File menu, and then click Print.

3. Click Advanced Print Settings.

4. Click the Publication Options tab.

5. Click to select the Improve Screen And Printer Color Matching check box.

6. Click OK.

7. Click Cancel to close the Print dialog box.

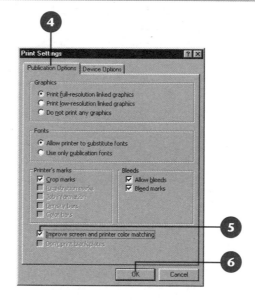

Adjusting Print Quality

As you lay out a publication, you may want to see what it looks like printed. Rather than print a high-quality version, try a *draft copy*. This lets you see the placement of elements and overall structure without waiting for the graphics to print and using extra toner or ink. Although you can change it later, you should set your printer and print resolution before you start. This way, you're sure that what you see on the screen is what you get in your printout. Changing midway might cause differences in the font size and appearance, character formatting, available paper sizes, printable page area, and print quality.

TIP

What dots? *Print resolution is measured in dots per inch (dpi). The more dots, the greater the resolution will be. 300 dpi is a fairly low resolution; 1200 dpi is a very high resolution.*

Print a Quick Draft Copy

1. Click the File menu, and then click Print.

2. Click Advanced Print Settings.

3. Click the Publications Options tab.

4. Click the Do Not Print Any Graphics option button.

5. Click OK.

6. Click OK.

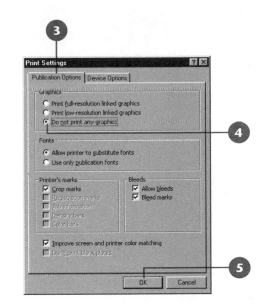

Set Print Resolution

1. Click the File menu, and then click Print.

2. Click Advanced Print Settings.

3. Click the Device Options tab.

4. Click the Resolution drop-down arrow, and then select a value.

5. Click OK.

6. Click OK.

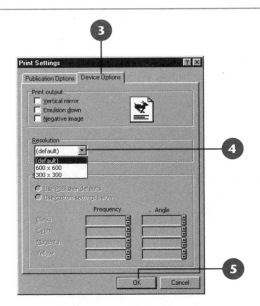

Using Special Paper

Do you want to impress clients and friends with a colorful design on letter-head, business cards, or invitations? Companies, like PaperDirect, produce colored or patterned papers that you can print on from your desktop printer. Publisher can display some of the most popular PaperDirect papers on the screen so you can see how your finished publication will look. When you print, only the text and graphics you added print, not the pattern. So you need to load your printer with the special paper.

TIP

Order PaperDirect.
PaperDirect is available on the Web. You can place an order, browse through paper styles, or order samples at www.paperdirect.com.

Adjust for Special Paper

1 Click the View menu, and then click Special Paper.

2 Click the pattern you want to print on.

To stop displaying a patterned paper, click None.

3 View the special paper pattern.

The description of the special paper appears in the Description area.

4 Click OK.

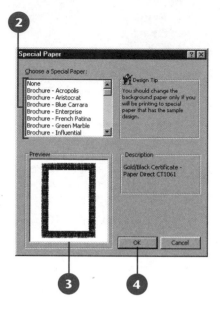

Print Business Cards

1. Open the publication with the business cards, click the File menu, and then click Print.

2. Click the Page Options button.

3. Click the Print Multiple Copies Per Sheet option button to print more than one card per sheet.

   If you used the Business Card Wizard, select the number of copies you want.

4. Click Custom Options.

5. Change the distance between cards, as needed.

6. Click OK.

7. Click OK.

8. Select print options as needed.

9. Click OK.

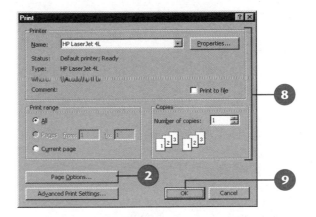

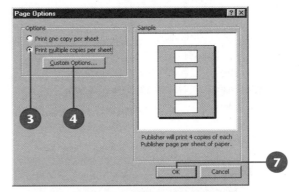

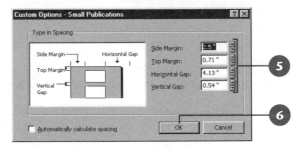

Printing Envelopes

Every letter you mail requires an envelope. To avoid retyping names and addresses, you can use mail merge to have Publisher address the envelopes for you. Then you need to ensure only that the text is placed on the envelope properly and that the envelope is oriented correctly for your printer. As you print, you might need to insert envelopes into the printer's sheet feed one at a time. Many desktop printers require you to manually feed an envelope into the printer.

SEE ALSO

See "Creating Merged Labels" on page 226 for information on laying out a label.

TIP

Return to the default settings. *Click to clear the Print Envelopes To This Printer Using These Settings check box to return to the default orientation and placement settings.*

Orient for Envelopes

1. Click the Tools menu, and then click Options.

2. Click the Print tab.

3. Click to select the Print Envelopes To This Printer Using These Settings check box.

4. Click an orientation option button.

5. Click a feed placement option button.

6. Click OK.

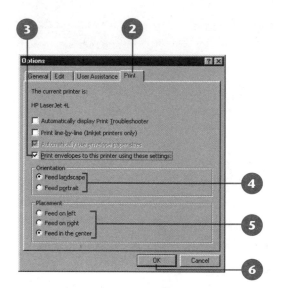

Print Envelopes

1. Click the File menu, and then click Print Setup.

2. If necessary, click the Name drop-down arrow, and then select a printer.

3. Click the Size drop-down arrow, and then select an envelope size.

4. Click the Source drop-down arrow, and then select Manual Feed (or Envelope Feed).

5. Click OK.

6. Click the Print button on the Standard toolbar.

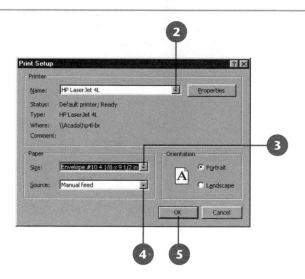

Printing Color Separations

You can choose two types of colors for your publication—spot color and process color.

Spot color is an individual color you apply to various elements or objects in your publication. Applying shading variations to those elements or objects makes them print in various tints of the spot color.

Process color mixes four basic ink colors (cyan, magenta, yellow, and black—or CMYK) to create all other colors. When you print color publications on a commercial printer, you need to supply the printer with a color separation as well as a composite.

What Are Color Separations?

Color separations are printouts that show where each color in your publication will print on that page. For every page in your publication, Publisher prints one separation for each color you used. If you use spot colors, each color is printed on its own page. If you use process colors, Publisher prints four pages—one for each of the four inks (cyan, magenta, yellow, and black). The separations show you and your printing service how each color is separated.

Separations aren't used to match colors, only to show how the colors will separate onto individual printing plates. Separations print in black and white even when you use a color desktop printer.

What Are Composites?

Composites are the exact opposite of separations. A *composite* combines all colors in a publication and prints them on one page. You can use a composite to review and verify the content of your publication. Because the composite shows all the design elements and content on one page, you can get a sense of the overall look and feel the publication conveys. Composites are also good for proofing. It's much easier to see errors in a printed copy than on the screen.

Commercial printers request color separations and composites so that they can see what your publication should look like as a whole, verify the print options and other settings are correct, and confirm that the colors are separated correctly.

Printing Separations or Composites

Before you print color separations, it's a good idea to run the Design Checker to catch any design problems. You should also verify that your publication is set up for color printing and the type of printer you plan to use.

1. Click the File menu, click Print, and select a printer.

2. To print a separation, click the Print Separations option button, and then select All to print all the separations (or select a color to print that one separation). To print a composite, click the Print Composite option button.

3. Click OK.

Trouble-shooting Printing Problems

Can't print? Fonts look weird? Graphics not printing? Layout doesn't look right? Printer error message? Whatever the problem, ask the Print Troubleshooter for help. The *Print Troubleshooter* provides step-by-step solutions for resolving common problems with desktop printing. Start by finding the description that most closely matches your problem. Then try the solution the Troubleshooter recommends. If that doesn't fix the problem, then move to the next possible solution. The solutions are listed with clear explanations of the possible reasons for the problem and step-by-step instructions to walk you through the most common printing problems.

Use Print Troubleshooter

1. Click the Help menu, and then click Print Troubleshooter.

2. Click the phrase in each window that most closely resembles your printing problem.

3. Follow the instructions step by step. If one set of the instructions does not solve the problem, continue with the next set.

4. When you're done, click the Close button.

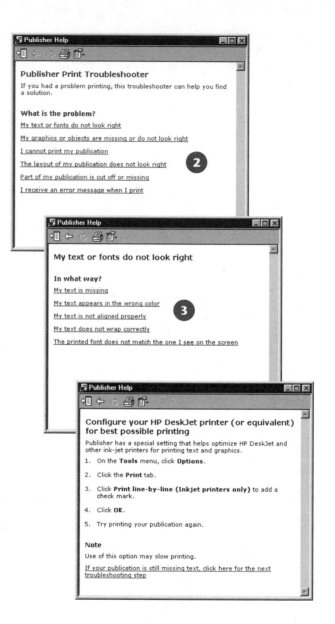

When Should You Use a Commercial Service?

Each of the three printing options—desktop printing, copy shop printing, and commercial printing—has advantages. You should consider several factors as you decide how to print your publication.

Turnaround Time

How quickly do you need your publication printed? Both desktop printing and copy shop printing can provide quick turnaround times. Some commercial printing services offer rush service, but this faster turnaround usually costs extra.

Quantity

How many copies do you need? You can print small jobs (fewer than 500 copies) economically at a copy shop. Some copy shops have digital printers that provide higher quality for smaller quantity printing at reasonable prices. For 500 or more copies, a commercial printing service is a good alternative.

Quality

Are you printing an informal publication, such as a flyer for a community event? If so, you probably don't need top quality and your desktop printer and copy shop duplication will do. However, if you're printing a marketing brochure for your company, then you'll likely want the high-resolution quality that commercial printing provides.

Color

Are you using color in your publication, such as color photographs or spot colors? If so, you can print the publication quickly with low- to medium-quality results on a desktop or copy shop color printer. For the highest color quality, however, take your publication to a commercial printing service.

Convenience

Do you want to use the most convenient and familiar way to do a job if it can be printed that way? Then you'll probably want to stick to your desktop printer or a copy shop. Do you have time to explore different methods that might offer higher quality and more options? If so, you may want to use a commercial printing service.

Cost

How much do you want to pay? Are you willing to pay more for the high-resolution color and quality offered by a commercial printing service? If not, then a copy shop or desktop printing is a better choice.

Setting Up for Color Printing

If you plan to print your publication with a commercial printer, you need to set up colors and printer's marks. First choose spot colors or process colors. If you decide to use spot colors, set up the colors you want for each spot color.

TIP

Use a custom spot color. *In the Choose Spot Color dialog box, click a Spot Color drop-down arrow, select More Colors, click All Colors, select a color model, and then click OK.*

TIP

How spot colors work. *If you choose black and one spot color, Publisher converts all colors except black to tints of the spot color. If you choose black plus two spot colors, only those objects that match the second spot color 100% print as the second color; all other colors print as tints of the first color.*

Choose Type of Color Printing

1 Click the Tools menu, point to Commercial Printing Tools, and then click Color Printing.

2 Click the type of color printing you want.

3 Click OK.

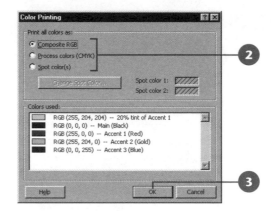

Set Spot Color

1 Click the Tools menu, point to Commercial Printing Tools, and then click Color Printing.

2 Click the Spot Color(s) option button.

3 Click Change Spot Color.

4 Click the Spot Color 1 drop-down arrow, and select a color.

5 If necessary, click the Spot Color 2 check box, and then select a second spot color.

6 Click OK.

7 Click OK.

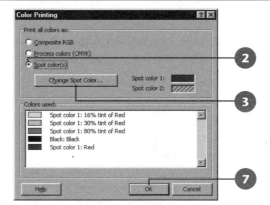

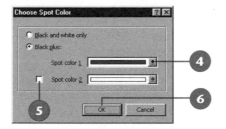

Printing with Crop and Registration Marks

Printer's marks are information outside the printable area on each page that shows where to trim, align, and control color. *Crop marks* are L-shaped marks that show where to trim (or cut) when the printed item is smaller than the paper size or align multiple pages when it is larger than one page. *Registration marks* show how to precisely align color separations.

TIP

Bars and marks. Color *and* density bars *monitor color on separations.* Job information *includes the publication name, page, print date and time, page number, and plate name.* Bleed marks *show where images, objects, or text extend beyond the page's trim.*

Turn On Crop Marks and Registration Marks

1 Click the File menu, and then click Print.

2 Click Advanced Print Settings.

3 Click the Publication Options tab.

4 Click to select the Crop Marks check box.

5 Click to select the Registration Marks check box.

6 Click OK.

7 Click OK.

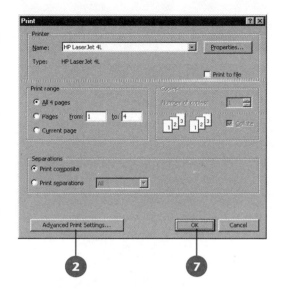

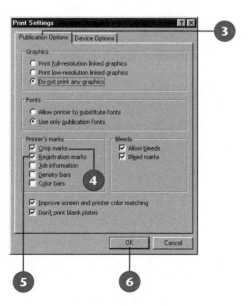

When to Use Knockouts or Overprinting

When colors overlap in selected items in your publication, you can decide how Publisher should treat the overlap. You can specify whether you want to use knockouts or overprinting for the items.

Suppose you create a surprise party invitation and want to make sure the word "Surprise!" stands out at the top of the party invitation. After you create the text of the invitation, you could format the "Surprise" text in big bold letters of one color and create a solid star shape of another color to go around it. When you overlap these two elements, the effect changes depending on whether you knock out the text or overprint the text.

Knockouts

Knockout is the process of removing the overlapping parts of a graphic or text from an element so that you can print those areas in a different color. Publisher knocks out color behind all foreground objects.

Consider the invitation heading, where the text is a golden yellow and the graphic is midnight blue. If you knock out the text from the star shape, then the golden "Surprise!" appears in a blue star. Both colors retain their original vibrancy and depth because they do not mix during the printing process.

Overprinting

Overprinting is the process of printing an element of one color over an element of another color without removing, or knocking out, the material underneath. By default, Publisher overprints black lines, fills, imported pictures, and black text (provided the text is smaller than the size specified in the overprint text setting) when these objects have a black percentage greater than or equal to the overprint threshold value. This means that objects must be darker than the value you set in order to overprint another color.

Consider the invitation heading with the golden yellow text and midnight blue graphic. If you overprint these colors, then the golden "Surprise!" will also show the blue ink from behind it. Instead, you might want to swap the colors of the two elements and overprint the darker color onto the lighter color so that the blue "Surprise!" jumps out of a yellow star.

You can turn off overprinting for black lines, fills, and imported graphics that cannot be color separated or that have been recolored to black in Publisher, and change minimum text size for overprinting.

Working with Trapping

Publisher provides an advanced commercial printing tool called *trapping* (overlapping edges of different colors). For example, if a text character overlaps dark, light, and similar-color backgrounds, Publisher traps each section of the character against each different background color. By default, trapping is turned off when a publication is created. You can turn on trapping and use Publisher's default settings, or you can override the default settings. Publisher only creates traps when printing separations. To print separations, the publication must first be set up for process-color or spot-color printing.

SEE ALSO

See "Setting Up for Color Printing" on page 240 for information on setting up for process-color and spot-color printing.

Change Trapping Preferences

1. Click the Tools menu, point to Commercial Printing Tools, point to Trapping, and then click Preferences.

    Check with your commercial printer for the specific trapping options you need.

2. Click to select the Automatic Trapping check box.

3. Click to select the specific trapping and black overprinting check boxes you want.

4. Click OK.

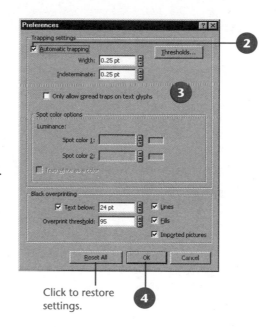

Click to restore settings.

Set Trapping for an Object

1. Select the object for which you want to set trapping.

2. Click the Tools menu, point to Commercial Printing Tools, point to Trapping, and then click Per Object Trapping.

3. Click a drop-down arrow, and then select the trapping option you need.

4. Click Close.

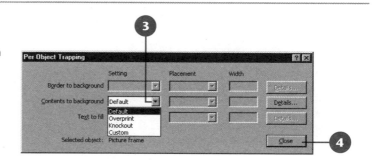

14

Embedding Fonts

To print your publication, your printing service must have the same fonts installed on their computer that you used in your publication. When you use TrueType fonts, Publisher can embed them with your publication. To ensure your printing service has the same fonts, embed the fonts in your publication. Although you can use Postscript and other non TrueType fonts in your publication, you cannot embed them in your publication.

TIP

Embed only part of a font.
Click the Tools menu, point to Commercial Printing Tools, click Fonts, click to select the Subset Fonts When Embedding check box, and then click OK.

SEE ALSO

See "Sending a Publisher File to a Printer" on page 248 for information on using the Pack And Go command to embed fonts.

Embed or Don't Embed a Font

1. Click the Tools menu, point to Commercial Printing Tools, and then click Fonts.

2. Click the font you want to change.

3. Click Embed or Don't Embed.

4. Click OK.

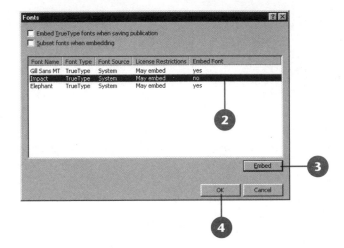

Choosing a Printer Driver

A *printer driver* is the device that tells Publisher what the selected printer can do, and tells the printer how to print your publication. To ensure that your publication prints correctly, you should install the printer driver for the printer where you'll do your final printing. You installed the appropriate drivers for your desktop printer when you loaded Windows. If you plan to use a commercial printer, you should install the PostScript printer driver and description file the printer recommends before you create your publication. Publisher includes two printer drivers that work with nearly all PostScript printers used by commercial printers (Imagesetter printer driver and Color Printer driver).

Choose a Printer Driver

1. Click the File menu, and then click Print Setup.

2. Click the Name drop-down arrow, then click the printer you will use for final output.

3. Click OK.

Install a Printer Driver

1. Click the Start button, point to Settings, and then click Printers.

2. Double-click the Add Printer icon, and then click Next.

3. Click the Local Printer or Network Printer option button, and then click Next.

4. Click the printer manufacturer and model you want to install, and then click Next.

5. Click the appropriate port, and then click Next.

6. Type a name for the printer, choose your default printer, and then click Next.

7. Click Finish.

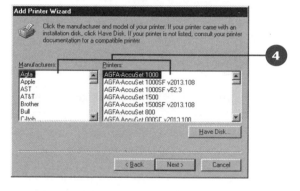

14

Creating a PostScript File

Most commercial printers work with PostScript (PS) files and Encapsulated PostScript (EPS) files. A PostScript file is used only for printing. Because you can't open or edit a PostScript file, make sure your publication is exactly the way you want it before you save it as a PostScript file. An Encapsulated PostScript file is a graphic of a single page of your publication. You can open, edit, and print an EPS file in many graphics programs. You need to create a separate EPS file for each page of your publication. You can't create an EPS file in Windows NT, only Windows 95 or later.

Save a Publication as a PostScript File

1. Click the File menu, and then click Save As.

2. Click the Save In drop-down arrow, and select a location in which to save the file.

3. Type a filename.

4. Click the Save As Type drop-down arrow, and then click PostScript.

5. Click Save.

6. Click the Name drop-down arrow, and then click a PostScript printer.

7. Click the Print Separations or Print Composite option button.

8. Click Advanced Print Settings, click the appropriate options on the Publications Options tab and the Device Options tab, and then click OK.

9. If available, click Page Options (or Tile Printing Options), choose settings, and click OK.

10. Click Save.

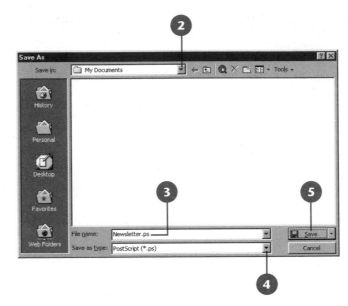

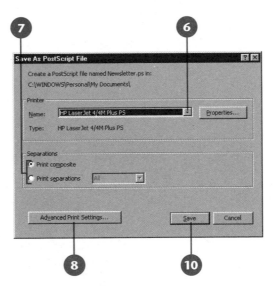

No PostScript preview. *You can't preview your PostScript file in Publisher. If you make changes to your publication after saving it as a PostScript file, you must create another PostScript file.*

Optimize for portability. *Windows optimizes PostScript for speed rather than portability. If you need to transfer many files to a commercial printer, you might want to change this option. Click the File menu, click Print Setup, click Properties, click Document Options, click PostScript Options, and click the Page Independence Option or the PostScript Output option to select it.*

Create an EPS file for each page of your publication. *You need to repeat the procedure for creating an EPS file for each page of your publication, one at a time. When you're done, copy all the EPS files for one publication to a disk for transferring.*

Save a Page as an EPS File

1. Click the View menu, and then click Two-Page Spread to deselect it.

2. Click the File menu, and then click Print Setup.

3. Select a PostScript printer.

4. Click Properties.

5. Click the PostScript tab.

6. Click the PostScript Output Format drop-down arrow, and then click Encapsulated PostScript (EPS).

7. Click OK in each dialog box.

8. Click the File menu, and then click Print.

9. Click to select the Print To File check box.

10. Click the Current Page option button.

11. Click the Print Composite option button.

12. Click OK.

13. Type a filename with .EPS as the extension in the File Name box in the Print To File dialog box.

14. Click OK.

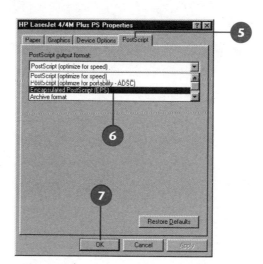

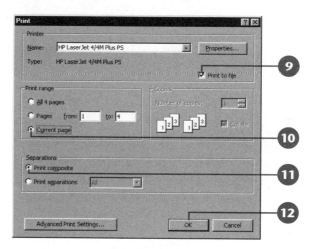

Sending a Publisher File to a Printer

To print your publication, a commercial printer needs your publication as well as any fonts and graphics you used in the publication. You can hand off your publication in Publisher format or PostScript format. If you hand off a Publisher file, Publisher verifies the graphics links, embeds fonts, and packs all the files the printer needs. Then the printer does a "preflight check," verifying fonts and linked graphics, trapping and correcting colors, and setting print options. If you hand off a PostScript file, you must do all these tasks yourself.

When Publisher packs your files, it embeds any TrueType fonts in your publication to ensure that the printer can display and print the fonts correctly. For any pictures, Publisher checks the links to the source files. If the source file is missing, you can update the link to the original picture or skip the picture so your printer can replace it with a different one.

The printer also needs a composite (all the colors in your publication printed on one sheet) and color separations (each color in your publication printed on a separate sheet). Publisher can print these on your desktop printer at the end of the packing sequence.

You can save your packed files to any directory you want. Publisher compresses and divides your files so they fit on individual disks; names and numbers the packed files; and adds a .puz extension. For example, your packed publication becomes Packed01.puz, Packed02.puz, and so on. The Unpack.exe program unpacks the files.

Pack Your Publisher Publication

After you finalize your publication, the Pack And Go Wizard collects, verifies, and packs your files, so you can bring them to the printer.

1. Click the File menu, point to Pack And Go, and then click Take To A Commercial Printing Service.

2. Click Next to continue.

3. Select the location for saving—an external drive, a floppy drive, or the hard disk, and then click Next to continue.

4. To embed TrueType fonts, include linked graphics and create links for embedded graphics. Click to select the Embed TrueType Fonts, Include Linked Graphics, and Create Links For Embedded Graphics check boxes, and then click Next to continue.

5. Click Finish.

6. If the source file for a linked graphic is missing, click Skip to leave the current link and replace the graphic later, or click Browse to locate the graphic.

7. If a message appears that you used fonts that can't be embedded, click OK and tell your printer.

8. Insert disks as necessary, and then click OK.

9. Click to select or clear the Print Separations and Print A Composite check boxes, and then click OK.

Index

Author's Acknowledgments

Robin Romer founded Pale Moon Productions in 1993 to help shed some light on the sometimes confusingly dark path to understanding software and technology. She specializes in writing and editing books about computer applications and technology, including the Microsoft Office suite, Netscape Navigator, PageMaker, the Internet, and Help Desks.

Acknowledgments Thanks to my husband, Brian Romer, who made sure I ate, slept, and laughed during this project. Lisa Ruffulo at the Software Connection, thank you for always suggesting the perfect edits. Also, thank you to Steve Johnson, David Beskeen, and the rest of the At a Glance team for providing that extra support when I needed a helping hand. I enjoy working with such a great group of people.

Elizabeth Eisner Reding has authored many computer books since 1992. Some of the topics include HTML, and Microsoft's Excel, PowerPoint, and Publisher products. She has worked for many publishers in the capacities of author, technical editor, and development editor. In her copious spare time, she collects fine art, renovates her home, and is working on a MBA degree.

Acknowledgments I'd like to thank the outstanding team responsible for making this book possible: my editor, Lisa Ruffolo; the copyeditor, Jane Pedicini; and Steve Johnson and David Beskeen at Perspection. What a great team!

I'd also like to thank my wonderful husband, Michael, for putting up with me when I was at my worst. What a sweetheart—and to think I was lucky enough to meet you on the "T"!

Marie Swanson has authored more than 30 books, including *Microsoft Access 97 At a Glance*, and Microsoft Word 6.0, Word 95, and Word 97 *Step by Step* books (Microsoft Press). With 17 years experience in corporate PC support and training environments, Marie and her company, WriteWorks, have written customized training materials and end-user documentation for internal accounting systems and image retrieval applications, as well as for major software packages.

Acknowledgments In addition to my assistants who provide valuable support, I would like to thank Lisa Ruffulo at the Software Connection and Jane Pedicini for their insightful editorial contributions. Of course, the greatest thanks must go to the people at Perspection, Inc., who provided me the opportunity to work on this project and who shepherded the entire process.

The manuscript for this book was prepared and submitted to Microsoft Press in electronic form. Text files were prepared using Microsoft Word 97 for Windows 95. Pages were composed in PageMaker for Windows, with text in Stone Sans and display type in Stone Serif. Composed pages were delivered to the printer as electronic files.

Cover Design
Tim Girvin Design

Graphic Layout
David Beskeen

Compositors
Gary Bellig
Tracy Teyler

Proofreader
Jane Pedicini

Indexer
Michael Brackney
Savage Indexing Service